Kathleen McCorm___ ___ ___ ___ ___
psychic, is descended from a Cornish family that
includes an ancestress who is alleged to have been
drowned for practising witchcraft.

Her Cornish grandfather (whose family originated
in Brittany) was taken to Australia as a small child,
and it was he who passed on his psychic gifts to
Kathleen's mother. He also followed the customary
Cornish occupation of mining and opened and
worked the first gold mines in Wyalong, New South
Wales.

There is a tradition in Kathleen McCormack's
family that the child of each generation who inherits
"the powers" invariably has orange-tawny eyes.
Like Kathleen and her youngest son . . .

Since her first book, *Fortune-Telling*, was published
in Fontana in 1972, Kathleen McCormack has lived
in England, where she is also a professional singer.

Tarot

Kathleen McCormack

Fontana/Collins

First published by Fontana Books 1973
Second Impression December 1974

© Kathleen McCormack 1973

Made and printed in Great Britain by
William Collins Sons & Co Ltd Glasgow

Contents

Introduction

"Let No Man Enter This Place, Save His Hands Be Pure".

That quotation, inscribed over the entrance to the temple of Apollo guarding the cave of the Delphic Oracle, gave some indication of the attitude displayed by the ancient Greeks towards the priests, priestesses and sibyls whose oracular utterances in the form of advice and prophecy were regarded as direct messages from the divine gods, and their messengers sacrosanct.

In ancient Rome, the establishment of the College of Augurs, whose priests predicted events by the practice of studying the habits of birds, elevated soothsaying to a semi-divine status. Other practices in the ancient world included the study of natural phenomena, the entrails of animals, the pattern of lightning flashes and the interpretation of dreams. Those who were fortunate enough to have acquired an education mastered the age-old science of astrology, and many a wealthy Roman family employed a personal astrologer or consulted a seer regularly. Both of these categories of people would have been regarded as possessors of an unusual but nevertheless recognised and accepted ability, and accorded respect for their skills.

It is only comparatively late in our history, when the early Christian Church was struggling to maintain its hold in Europe by stamping out all traces of the old religion, that Saturn became confused with Satan; and the word witch, deriving from the Wicce, the wise or all-seeing, gained the connotation of godlessness and evil. From there, it was but a short step from nature-worship to devil-worship, and the seers, those gifted with pre-natural insight, became obscured in a cloud of fear and superstition.

So, for many centuries, psychic abilities lay under a cloud. It was something which the frightened possessor regarded as being from the Devil himself, or, in the hardier souls, lay accepted but undisclosed for fear of persecution. In the latter so-called "Age of Rerson", it was often regarded as something which must be kept well hidden for fear of ridicule. It is only in the last forty years that an open interest has been evinced in the occult, and great advances made in the study of the mysterious powers of the mind, although for twice that number of years psychic and spiritualist societies had been conducting experiments with striking but little publicised results. The scientific methods of Dr Rhine at Duke University in America have proved conclusively that there exists a telepathic ability termed extra sensory perception, and also that hand in hand with this sense, there is another which incorporates the ability to look into the future and sometimes to look backwards into the past. These have not, as yet, been fully explained, but the results have been so conclusive, the tests so fool-proof and the methods so scientific, that they cannot be ignored, dismissed or laughed away as many older conclusive experiments were.

Let's call it, for want of a better description, the sixth sense – which it may very well be. I believe it to be present in a large percentage of the population in varying degrees, but in most cases awaiting development and guidance to enable it to be used properly. For some psychics, this sense is so over-whelmingly strong, there is no need for such devices as cards, cups or crystal balls which are, basically, a method of trancing the mind or a guideline for the intuition. For it is when the mind's mental activity is quietened, and the point of focus set, that the intuition or the sixth sense fed by the supra-conscious comes into play. The symbols of the cards or tea leaves act as guide lines for the messages which come through clairvoyantly.

The most fascinating, bewildering and mysterious of these divinatory aids are the ancient Tarot cards. Their meanings rise high above mundane material existence. They are concerned with the less transitory values, the more important moral triumphs and failures that make up man's progress through life. Their spiritual significance lifts them above the mere fortune-telling device. Their accent is on spiritual growth, evolution, Karmic forces and cosmic consciousness, and must never be approached in a spirit of levity or used for selfish personal gain.

Everything about them is intriguing and mysterious, from their unknown sources, their purpose, their underlying philosophy, their history, even to the origin of their name. These have all been subjects of many conflicting and confusing theories, written by learned authorities for nearly two hundred years.

I hope, in this book, not to further confuse the reader, for I am not adding anything new to the study of Tarot. Rather I am hoping to give a concise and simplified account of the history, the different authors and readers, the possible origin of the symbology, the collective meanings of the twenty-two picture cards of the Major Arcana and the fifty-six suit cards of the Minor Arcana, and basic easy methods of divination for the layman who wants to learn as much as he can about the Tarot cards in the shortest time and in terms he can understand. I am indebted to many authorities for the material collected and have gained experience, over many years as a clairvoyant, in the methods of divination, but humbly consider myself still a student of the Tarot, for the more I learn, the more there is to learn about these fascinating cards. At the back of the book I have placed a list of books on various aspects of the Tarot for those who wish to pursue the subject further.

Introduction
The History of the Tarot

On the stage of mediaeval Europe, paganism still postured
from behind a variety of masks and disguises. Although the
Christian Church had adopted many of its rituals and trans-
formed many of its beliefs, it kept a wary eye on certain
practices considered godless and suspect. One of these was
gambling, for luck was still equated in many men's minds
with the pagan god Lok, and the Church distrusted the pagan
appeal that fate or Kismet made to the senses. All forms of
gambling were abhorred but particularly that of card playing.
It is an interesting pointer that the word sorcery came from
the Latin word to cast lots and the Semitic word for sorcery
'naib' derived from the word meaning card play or gambling.
This attitude still lingered in the days of the Puritans who,
sensing the pagan defiance behind the Tarot imagery, called
it 'the Devil's picture book'.

The first recorded diatribe against card play is attributed
to a monk at Brefeld, Switzerland, in 1377. This seems by
description to refer not to the picture cards of the 22 Major
Arcana trumps or 'triumphs' as they were called, but to a
pack of fifty-six suit cards, the derivation of our modern
pack of gambling cards. It is thought that the two packs were
amalgamated at a later date, and not until 1450, by the
writings of another monk, a Franciscan friar in Northern
Italy, was the entire set referred to in yet another exhortation
against the evils of gambling and the pagan imagery of the
picture cards.

The earliest recorded purchase of cards was found in the
ledgers of the Dukedom of Brabant in 1379 and in the
same year card play was described at a fête in Brussels, but
the fullest description of a purchase of three packs of cards
was made by the court treasurer of Charles VI of France in
1392. They had been commissioned by a famous artist thought
to be Gringonneur, and were painted on vellum, edged with
gold and covered with silver, lapis lazuli and a dark red pig-

ment fancifully called 'mummy's dust'. Seventeen cards thought to be from this set in the Bibliotheque Nationale in Paris are now considered to be of a later manufacture.

Although cards were banned in Regensburg, Germany, as early as 1378, such was their universal appeal that by 1380 they were permitted by the Code of Nuremburg, and by 1393 were listed as among the permitted games in Florence. However, the hard-headed French passed a ban in Paris in 1397, preventing commoners from gambling with cards on working days. A typically English decree came later in England, in 1463, passed by an equally hard-headed King Edward IV. This was not to ban card playing but to prohibit imports of cards from foreign countries, such a commercial success had they become. By this time, master card-makers had appeared for the first time in the Brabant guild registers and women card-painters were known to be registered at Nuremburg. This industry had become possible by the introduction of wood block printing in Europe in the early fifteenth century and saw the end of the flimsy cheap stencilled packs. The wealthier section of the community had always been in the practice of commissioning artists to design Tarot packs, and indeed many famous artists found time in the midst of their larger commissions to create their own card packs. Dürer came to Italy, saw the Minchiate pack and upon his return to Germany produced his own version. It is a fascinating thought that today we still have some of these mediaeval designs, for the almost unaltered Marseilles pack was based on early wood-cuts.

Preserved from the wrath of St Bernardin of Sienna, who made a public proclamation against cards in 1423, and doubtless consigned many such exquisite packs to the flames in righteous wrath, the Visconti pack, created by Marziona de Tartona for Fillipo Marie Visconti, the Duke of Milan, is perhaps the most famous of all traditional Tarot packs known today. Many other packs were designed for the great dynastic families of northern Italy, and one such, the Bologna, was probably the object of St Bernardin's indignation. It was designed by Francesco Fibbia, the Prince of Pisa, during his exile in Bologna, and is said by some to be the originator of the Tarot pack in its present form. However, it contained no Minor Arcana under six, (a practice that many fortune-tellers even today follow) and was called the *Tarochinno* or little Tarot pack and obviously designed for a game of his own invention. The Visconti pack, it is said, copied his conception but added the missing numeral cards. Certainly the Prince of Pisa was given great honours and it is suggested that he received them for his idea of combining the suit cards with an older pack of picture cards, used perhaps for some purpose other than gambling, or invented the Tarot symbols themselves, using something else as a model. His symbolism was striking, the Major Arcana seemingly denoting man's spiritual progress in material existence, and his sequence culminated at 'the Judgement', giving force to this moralistic theme. Yet again there is another opinion which concerns the four Tarot cards in the Musée Carrer which are thought not to be French as accepted, but Venetian, and these are considered by some to be the parents of all the other packs.

Another Italian pack is the Florentine or Minchiate pack. This consists of the regular seventy-eight Tarot cards, plus the twelve astrological signs, the four basic elements, earth, air, fire and water, and the four virtues, faith, hope, charity, and prudence.

These three Italian packs form the basis of the modern Tarot packs available today. There are many different packs, – some national, such as the French Marseilles pack; German and Swiss which carry for the suit devices bells, acorns, roses and shields; some from the Psychic Institute and various spiritual orders; the Etteilla Tarot; and the Pamela Coleman Smith cards designed for Waite, influenced by Rosicrucian doctrine.

However, there is one pack in existence, known as the Baldini pack, but once thought to have been executed by Mantegna, which differs in many ways from the accepted Tarot and was considered to have been used as a memory system in a quasi-theological game during a seven month Ecclesiastical Council in 1459, to relieve the tedium for the Pope and his two Cardinals. This set made free use of pagan symbology, and consisted of fifty cards of five denaries of ten cards each, embracing in picture form the conditions of life, the liberal arts and sciences, the virtues, the heavens and the muses. One authority, Romain Merlin, asserted that this set dated from the fourteenth century and others copied and diverged from it. It has certain similarities with the pack designed for Charles VI of France, and Merlin's view was that Tarot cards were well known in Europe long before Gringonneur designed this set for the French king. However, as we have learned before, it has now been established that the seventeen cards thought to be from this early French set are considerably later in period and of possible Italian origin.

The Baldini pack is interesting because it is said to represent a mnemonic system, and this type of memory aid is said by Paul Huson, a leading modern authority on the occult, to have been the original purpose of the Major Arcana. This theory seems to me more acceptable than many high-flown esoteric explanations given in the past for the conception of the Tarot, but the arguments make fascinating reading so let us trace the confusing and conflicting theories of scholars from the discovery of these cards up to the present day.

The Theories

In one of the nine works of a massive volume, *Le monde primitif*, French writer Antoine de Gébelin, amateur scholar, antiquarian and historian, wrote in 1781 a section called 'Le Jeu de Tarots', dealing with the Tarot cards. The author had come across these a few years earlier, and had become excited by their symbology which he attributed to the occult beliefs of ancient Egypt. He was interested in everything pertaining to ancient Egypt, as were many scholars of the neo-classical period, and as the Rosetta Stone was not to be discovered for another eighteen years, he was safe to assert that these cards were the remains of the sacred Book of Thoth. He discovered that the cards were relatively unknown in France, except in the southern country districts and Marseilles, but that they were of considerable antiquity and had existed in Belgium, Italy, Germany and Spain, both as a divinatory method and as a game of chance, for hundreds of years. He studied the methods, and the attributed meanings, but reconstructed the cards, altering some of the symbolism and the meanings to fit in with both his Egyptian theory and his philosophy as a high grade Mason.

A contemporary of his and disciple, Alliette, or Etteilla, as he later respelled his name, a Parisian barber, published his own work on the Tarot two years after de Gébelin's, and further accentuated the divinatory aspect of the cards. His knowledge of the occult was mere surface gleanings compared to de Gébelin's, and he lacked the other's spirituality, but he possessed a strong commercial sense and a flair for showmanship. He became one of the foremost fortune-tellers in France. He styled himself 'priest of the occult' and produced two more books which were written, he claimed, by seventeen Magi of the Temple of Fire on the borders of the Levant. His books appealed to the masses but the pack of cards he produced, which is still in use today, is considered by many later authorities to have been a debased version of de Gébelin's. Although he claimed that his innovations were but corrections of the inevitably corrupted Egyptian designs, they are said to be a tasteless amalgamation of contemporary French emblems and traditional symbols. He added nothing new to the solution of the Tarot mystery, merely promoting the Egyptian theory and adding his own rather suspect designs and interpretations of the meanings.

The newly-awakened interest in these cards resulted naturally in a spate of fortune-tellers, although there had been books published on fortune-telling in France as early as 1634, using cards and dice. After Etteilla came two more renowned seers, both authors. They were Julia Orsini and Marie le Normand. The latter achieved renown by her prediction of Napoleon's marriage to Josephine, and later published a book claimed to be based on papers left with Mademoiselle le Normand by the same Josephine. Her methods were quite unique, and she is said to have needed only three cards on which to base an entire reading. Claiming among her clients such personages as the Tzar of Russia, she was greatly in demand and accordingly set her fees very high. She published a book on card reading methods and created her own pack based loosely on the Tarot. These can be purchased today, and some of her methods are still used.

Then came a wave of more rational scholars who disagreed with the rather romantic Egyptian theory. One Samuel Singer echoed another earlier Italian writer, Covelluzo, who claimed in his book written in the fifteenth century, that the cards entered Italy from Arabia in the fourteenth century. Two more dissenters were Duchesne and William Chatto, who agreed that the Tarot was European in origin and the Egyptian theory high-flown romance.

Next, an interesting suggestion developed into a contra-theory when P. B'Oiteau D'Ambley wrote a treatise on playing cards and identified the Tarot with the Bohemian gypsies, after detecting what he considered to be a slight oriental influence. This he attributed to the transit of the gypsies through India on their way to Europe. Three years later a more formidable exponent of the Roman theory, J. A. Vaillant, who had lived with the gypsies and was considered to be a leading authority on the Romany language, history and culture, wrote a book suggesting that the Tarot originated with the gypsies. Later scholars seem to be of the opinion that although the Romanies may have spread the divinatory lore of the Tarot through our Europe from a very early time, there is little evidence to support Vaillant's assertions. Romain Merlin, in 1869, refuted this theory by stating that the Tarot cards were in existence in Europe long before the arrival of the gypsies, which is recorded as 1417 at Luneberg. However, there are indications that wandering tribes of Romanies were familiar in Europe long before that date, and it is an interesting fact that the Romany word for deck of cards is Tar. This is even more striking when we find that the language of these people derives from the purest form of Sanskrit, itself the oldest of the Indo-European languages and the same word in the old language is Taru. The ancient belief that the Romanies came from Egypt (our English word gypsy derives from the word Egyptian), is thought-provoking according to one brilliant authority, Paul Huson. He points out that the patron saint of the Romanies, Saint Sara, has her shrine, Les Saintes Maries de la Mer, in the Camargue, and this rests upon what legend has it is the site of an ancient altar of the Roman god Mithras. Mithras assimilated the Egyptian god of the dead into his pantheon, and that god's name was Sarapis. According to another modern writer, Wenzell Brown, the gypsies have always claimed that they possess a secret book more ancient than any known, which is the only true guide to fortune-telling by the cards. No copy of this has ever come to light, and it seems that the divinatory methods of the gypsies are handed down in an oral tradition. The same author states that in his belief some version of the Tarot cards were the tablets (referred to in the Book of Moses) which the Israelites consulted.

But again, a hundred years ago, all roads seemed to lead back to ancient Egypt, and the next scholar who published his works in the middle of the last century sustained this theory, embellished by additions of his own. He could be said to have shaped the modern attitude to the Tarot – or at least that which prevailed up to the last thirty years. He was Alphonse Constant, better known as Eliphas Levi. First educated in a Catholic order and destined for the Church, he later switched to a study of the occult and published works on magic – aspects of which linked with the Tarot trumps the Major Arcana. His contribution to the subject was to link the meanings of the Tarot trumps with the Hebrew mystical system, first known in Spain in the twelfth century as the Qabbala. He also linked each Tarot trump with the letters of the Hebrew alphabet, each of which has a mystical meaning, and the emblems of the four suits, as well as the four elements fire, water, earth and air, and the four Hebraic symbols of the divine name, Yod, Heh, Vau and Yahveh. He considered the cards a key to ancient magic, and influenced by Vaillant, later considered them to have been introduced into Europe by the gypsies. In turn, another later occultist, Oswald Wirth, designed a pack of cards based on Levi's ideas, but Levi's greatest exponent was Papus who published the *Tarot of the Bohemians* in the 1890s. This work incorporated Wirth's cards with Levi's theories and added a new dimension of meaning to the Minor Arcana, based on the Hebrew system of numbers. He introduced as a basis for the meanings of these cards a system of threes; commencement, apogee and decline. He also edited Etteilla's earlier work on Tarot – thus saving it from oblivion. Papus, a doctor of medicine, a Rosicrucian, and founder of a school of the occult in Paris, believed that the Major Arcana embodied the spiritual history of man; or the soul of man, coming out from the eternal, passing through material darkness, and emerging into the light again.

Another school of thought evolving in England about this time was due to the foundation of a Rosicrucian type order, 'The Order of the Golden Dawn'. This body correlated the Tarot cards with the Qabbalistic concept of the 'Tree of Life'. This is a mystical diagram of ten stages or aspects in ascending triangles linked together by twenty-two paths, thought of as the 'Anatomy of the Deity' and embracing such concepts as grace, mercy, serenity, victory, splendour and many more. The man largely responsible for this new development was Samuel Mathers, later known as McGregor Mathers, who published a book in which he propounded that the Tarot trumps were in their numerical sequence, a moral treatise on human will and enlightenment. He also incorporated the zodiac and the planets into his credo. This school of thought differed in the order of the cards, and some modern packs today diverge on this point. However, since the early cards differed again in numerical sequence, this is of little significance to the diviner. Whereas some authorities place the Fool at the end of the sequence, or do not number this card, this Order equates it with the Hebrew letter Aleph, the beginning, but number it 'O' – symbol of the eternal. Their pack, created for the members and not for general use, was based on the 'Tree of Life' and its gradations and meanings, allied with the Qabbala. A pack following these lines was published in 1916 by a member of this Order, A. E. Waite, a renowned scholar of the occult. With the help of artist Pamela Coleman Smith, herself a member of the Order of the Golden Dawn, he changed much of the traditional design of the Minor Arcana, by making them picture cards. Later scholars have criticized this departure from tradition, and also his incorporation of Rosicrucian concepts into the meanings of the cards. He re-edited *The Tarot of the Bohemians*, the older work by Papus, but had scant sympathy with the 'Book of Thoth' concept, and considered that although Papus was on the right track when he asserted that the Tarot was a collection of esoteric writings, he did not delve deeply enough. In his opinion, the Tarot symbology was universal, their truths to be found on two levels, and the divinatory aspects incidental and unimportant. His was the suggestion that the two packs were originally combined by the Prince of Pisa. Another view of his was that the symbols of the Minor Arcana are linked with the Holy Grail. Other scholars have noticed the similarity of these emblems with the Irish magical treasure, the spear of Lug, the cauldron of Dagda, the sword of Nuada and the stone of Fal, but Waite leans more to the Arthurian legends and says the spear of Lug could also be the spear of Longinus in the legend of the Holy Grail. Strangely, Eden Gray, who has written a manual for fortune-telling based on the Waite-Coleman Smith cards, completely reverses the order of the suits and their accepted tradition of denoting the colouring which indicates our choice of the significator card for the client. However, this is a small point, and the fact that Waite's meanings may differ slightly from the traditional Marseilles pack's interpretation does not really matter. His cards are very beautiful indeed, and helpful for the beginner as the imagery on the suit cards illustrates the basic meaning.

There were other books by members of this Order. One outstandingly different work was produced by Aleister Crowley after he had broken away from the Order of the Golden Dawn and founded his own Order of the Silver Star. This he called ambitiously *The Book of Thoth* and the only new contribution or improvement he made to those works produced by the members of his former Order was to change the order of progression of trumps to make a more convincing correlation with the 'Tree of Life' doctrine. A noted occultist of the 30's, P. Ouspensky, did not believe that the cards had any sequential relationship, but rather that each card must be contrasted with another. The Fool is contrasted with card number one, card number two with card number twenty-one, card number three with card number twenty and so on. A more modern writer, Sidney Bennett, links the court and other cards with astrology and the seasons. Numerology is also incorporated in this system of reading, by bringing the date of the day and the year to one unit, then linking it with all cards in the Major or Minor Arcana that carry that number. This author asserts that a similar cycle of events will occur on each number one day, (that is – a day of which the date plus the numerals of the year will reduce to the unit one, for instance the twelfth May 1973) (1 plus 2 plus 5 plus 1 plus 9 plus 7 plus 3 equals 28 equals 2 plus 8 equals 10 equals 1 plus 0 equals 1) and to obtain a forecast you simply check each morning all Major or Minor cards which carry that number, and read the divinatory meaning. Another modern author who relates the Tarot to the seasons and the zodiac is Carlyle A. Pushong, who also has some interesting correlations to make between the Tarot doctrine and Sankara's doctrine of Maya.

He also underlines the philosophy of reincarnation and Karma. Richard Gardner, a noted modern writer and occult scholar, believes that the Minor Arcana symbolizes the four elementals composing all manifestations, (fire, water, earth and air) in differing quantities according to their numerical value; and the Major Arcana gives us a pattern for living by showing us our hidden potential and the restrictions which prevent our succeeding. He believes that two dynamics motivate us and all around us; fire and water. Fire is equated always with the masculine religions and water with the feminine. These two elements react upon earth and air, and the four elements which we all have present within each of us must be balanced harmoniously in order for us to live happily and achieve our full potential. The suit of Cups he maintains is ruled by water; the Wands by fire; the Sword by air; and the Pentacle by earth.

The modern view, that the Tarot was a memory system used by one of the Gnostic sects, has been presented skilfully and convincingly by Paul Huson and discussed intelligently and sympathetically by Alfred Douglas, both brilliant modern authorities on the Tarot. This latter-day theory is the most fascinating of all in my opinion, and in many ways the most convincing. Possibly Harold Bayley first came to this conclusion when, examining a parchment of Albigensian origin, he noted that the Eucharistic symbol depicted thereon showed a remarkable resemblance to the symbol for the Ace of Cups of the Tarot. He concluded that the Tarot has evolved as a secret language of the Albigensian sect. But why secret, and what is Albigensian?

Again we have to return to mediaeval Europe and from there to the excitement of the Renaissance. A great revival of learning led to the classical past being rediscovered. Boundaries were widening in every way. New seaways were being discovered and travellers like Marco Polo had set the world record for distance and opened up a new world. Byzantium's influence was waning while the cities of northern Europe were dominating the trade routes. The Italian and Venetian ports were becoming great centres of commerce, busy bustling cities responsible for transporting armies, victualling the crusaders and accommodating within their walls many different nationalities. The Italian merchants now travelled as far as England, Russia and Spain, while the sea captains and traders learned first-hand of the strange customs and alien philosophies of China and India, and with the cargoes and the profits came new and disturbing ideas. This knowledge began to spread, and the multi-racial nature of the cities bred an interest in foreign lands and begat a tolerance that drew

20

scholars from every land to study at the centres of the new learning. A growing interest in the literature of other lands caused centres of translation to spring up in France and Spain, and scholars then for the first time had access to the philosophy and legends of many cultures. All kinds of subjects were translated, ranging from treatises on Arabian astrology to Christian writings, neo-Christian subjects, classical literature. Even a French version of the Arthurian legend found its way over the Channel. Pagan gods and goddesses, the heroes of legend and song, were permeating the literature of the period. This preoccupation with the classical, its philosophies and religious beliefs, seems to have sprung from a universal sense of failure. The established religions had not satisfied an inner hunger for spiritual development, and a consequent thirst for knowledge arose and with it came the search for more lasting values. The Gnostic sects had flourished in Alexandria as early as the second century A.D. They were breaks-offs from the orthodox Christian religions and were considered by the established church to be heretical servants of the Devil. The word Gnostic comes from the Greek work for knowledge, and this name was applied loosely to a number of separate sects, all of whom had descended from the Paulisians, an Armenian Christian heretical sect whose beliefs were a mixture of Persian, Chaldean, Indian, Egyptian, Hebrew and Christian beliefs, laced heavily with Greek philosophy. There were sects whose only real difference was regional and they were named after their location: for example as the Bogomils, and their off-shoots the Waldenses and the Albigenses, or as these were also designated, the Cathars. This last sect, whose name meant 'pure', were dualists who believed in two opposing forces for good and evil, Christ and the Demi-Urge. They rejected resurrection both of Christ and of themselves, and believed that the Demi-Urge created the body, in which is contained a Divine Spark, the godhead, or the opposing good, which can only be set free through knowledge and consequent enlightenment. The mediaeval Church, though not averse to borrowing some of the customs and emblems of these sects, endeavoured to stamp out all practices considered to be anti-Christian, and drove the Gnostics underground or exterminated them altogether.

With this suspicious attitude and rigid persecution of anything outside the teaching of the Church, the centres of learning narrowed down to the cloisters. Literacy was even among the wealthier classes, and most of the teaching lay in the hands of the clergy. Much of this pagan literature was consigned to the flames, but a considerable amount of the dangerous heretical works on magic was retained and studied by scholarly clerics with an occult bent. These gave the explanation or excuse that the Church must fully understand the older doctrines in order to know thoroughly the enemy it was fighting.

Such ancient magical works as *The Greater Key*, *The Book of Solomon*, *The Picatrix*, and the *Grimoires*, which described spells, gave instructions for the conjuring up of spirits, the controlling of demons and the fashioning of powerful magical talismans and found their way into the monasteries as well as books on alchemy and astrology. Because writing was a much prized but rare skill in these days there evolved a system of memory training in the form of a series of pictorial images arranged in a certain order. These were a kind of mental shorthand, each image itself a stimulus to release given information previously memorized. One section of opinion had long considered memory-aids a direct path to the Devil. St Thomas Aquinas condemned the *Ars Notoria*, a Mnemonic system, for both its pagan imagery and its underlying reliance on the powers of magic. The alchemist had considered memory training a stimulus to the unconscious, and the use of these techniques plus the intoning of certain magical formulae was considered a method of invoking the supernatural. One fragment of a memory system used in the monasteries still in existence today is the Stations of the Cross.

Paul Huson believes that the Tarot trumps may well have been some such memory system, deriving from a classical mystery cult, based on Isis and Hermes Trismegistos (known in Egypt as Thoth), that god that the Gnostics claimed was the originator of the twin sciences of alchemy and astrology.

There has been a view put forward that the Tarot cards were the invention of the Knights Templar. This was an ascetic military order founded by Hugh de Payens in 1188, with eight fellow knights, to protect pilgrims and guard routes to the Holy Land. However, over the centuries the Order had become extremely powerful and too wealthy. Philip XIV of France in 1307 brought charges of heresy against the Order, had many members tortured into making false confessions, confiscated their property and had their leader publicly burned at the stake. All the other centres in other countries were treated in a similar manner and the Order disbanded in 1314. It has been suggested that the Templars were worshipping a version of Mithras, the Roman ruler of the sun and war, and the natural divinity for a military order. One link with the Tarot cards is the eighteenth century portrayal of card number fifteen, the Devil, whose imagery is consistent with the Baphomet (the common word for any idol) supposedly worshipped by the Templars. Statues somewhat similar had been found in some of their meeting places, and considered by the Christian Church to represent the Devil, although they were derived from Janus and Saturn.

Another interesting theory on the creation of the Major Arcana takes us back to mediaeval Italy where a golden strand in the fabric of life in the Italian cities was the pageants and festival processions. These were called Triumphs and were often commissioned by one of the ruling princes, and could be in honour of a visiting dignitary or a Saint's day, or sometimes to celebrate a dynastic marriage, or again, to please the Church. Originally of a religious nature, possibly stemming from ancient mystery plays, they were usually dramatic tales with a moral theme. They developed into such costly and elaborate tableaux that artists were commissioned to design them and engineers to create the mechanism of animation. Leonardo da Vinci designed one such Triumph, and from the fourteenth century there existed a game using the twenty-two picture cards, called Triumphs. It is a possibility that the Tarot cards themselves may have been the commemoration in miniature of one such memorable procession, perhaps given by the artist to his wealthy patron, or commissioned by the patron himself, or perhaps they themselves were used as an integral part of the pageant or Triumph in long-ago Italy.

The Gambling Cards

I have left until this chapter a few other interesting views concerning the origin of the Tarot, because I think it is time we delved into the fascination of gambling and deal briefly with cards used for that purpose. Craftsmen and artists of every nation, for thousands of years, have produced little masterpieces in the interests of gambling, for the lure of luck, the element of risk attendant upon the flicking of a die or the turn of a card has been a universal attraction since time immemorial.

It is believed that card playing derives from the ancient practice of primitive tribes of throwing arrows into a hallowed or magical circle for the purpose of divination. In Korea, today, there exists a game called *Nyout* which derives from this ancient practice, common to other primitive peoples such as the American Indian, and the Korean cards, which are very long and thin, still bear an arrow stencilled on their backs.

Chess had its origin in a game played before the days of Troy by shepherds of western Asia. The game featured the use of pebbles in a divided square, with a sheepfold in the centre. From this game came both the later Roman game of draughts and a game known as *Petteia*, which gradually assumed a more military character and became the forerunner of our modern chess. Another ancient game, that of *Mora*, still played today and known to have been played in the time of Moses in ancient Egypt, may also have derived from *Petteia*; draught boards and gaming-boards were depicted on murals found in the tombs of the pharaohs, and one such tomb, that of Tutankhamen, in recent times, yielded up a beautiful example of a gaming-board of inlaid ivory and gold.

The game was possibly taken to China by a tribe of wandering Hindus, for it had long been known in Arabia, Persia and India in its original form. They gave it a unique Chinese character which it retains to this day, for they settled across the river from the fierce marauding Tartars, and the Chinese chessboard still shows a space in the middle of the board representing this river or barrier, while the chess pieces mirror the warlike character of the protagonists.

Papus noticed a similarity between the 'coat' or court cards, so named for their elaborate robes, and some of the chess pieces, such as the kings and queens, the tower, the bishop and the knave. He also commented upon the fact that the earlier boards the Crusaders brought back with them had numbered squares which early philosophers had used to solve problems of logic. He thought that if the numbers were separated and made into a die and the pictured trumps placed around a wheel, we should then have the game of *Goose* with which Ulysses practised cheating beneath the walls of Troy. It may well have been *Petteia* Ulysses played, but the game of *Goose* was of much later origin.

B'Oiteau D'Ambley's theory that the Tarot had an oriental origin, having been brought by the Romans to Europe via India, is true in one particular. So may be the observation by Papus, of the similiarity of the Tarot with the chess pieces denoting a common origin for the Tarot is thought to have been based on an amalgamation of Chinese chess pieces and gambling cards. These are the earliest known cards in existence, and date back to the eleventh century. The cards were apparently based on the design of paper money which had been introduced into China in the T'ang dynasty, some time between 600 A.D. and the end of the tenth century. Marco Polo remarked upon this paper money, which was later copied by Venetian and Italian traders who brought it back to Europe. Apparently real money was used sometimes in China in these games. Cards in China were also interchangeable with dominoes, the latter being used for fortune telling and decorated with different flowers, animals and folk heroes. Possibly the cards and dominoes were brought to Europe, and the card makers adapted and Europeanized the Chinese signs and symbols without knowing their significance, resulting in the traditional suit signs and our court cards.

There has also been a vague suggestion that the Tarot could have an Indian origin. This was based on the Romany theory and the fact that there could be a slight analogy between the Cups relating to priests or Brahmins, the Swords to the warrior, the Coins to the merchants, and the Batons to the serfs or peasants. The Major Arcana, it was observed, had certain similarities with the divine concepts of Buddha. However, these delineations of Cups, Wands, Deniers and Swords, could just as well apply to the different strata of mediaeval Italy, or as we have seen to the Grail Hallows, and the symbology of the Tarot could be considered universal. There is now a view that Indian playing cards actually derived from the European cards, and that their circular shape may have come from their original interchangeability with chess pieces, as in China. The Indian cards have eight or ten suits, and their symbology, which is mainly religious, derives from the ten reincarnations of Vishnu.

Samuel Singer, in the nineteenth century, stated that *Trappolo* was the earliest game played in Europe and was introduced by the Arabs, by way of Italy. Covelluzo, however, writing in the fifteenth century, stated that the Saracens introduced the game *Naib* into Italy in 1379 when the rival Popes, Clement VII and Urban VI, engaged mercenaries from Arabia to fight in their private armies. However, Arabs had been living in Spain as early as the eighth century, had also been in Italy before 1379 and had penetrated before that time as far as Arles in France and into Sicily. This theory comes up against those experts who point out that, if cards did originate in Arabia, it is odd that there is no mention of them in *The Arabian Nights*. Of course it is possible that cards were banned, but it is strange that such a forbidden and alluring pastime would not somewhere form the basis of a tale of delight and punishment. In any case, the Saracens' Muslim religion forbade both gambling and drawing human figures, so it is unlikely that the Tarot originated with them.

Singer says that the Semitic word for card play is *naipes*, the derivation of our 'Jack O'Napes', and it is a fact that the ancient game of *Roccambo*, played in Spain, used the Tarot suits; but the word *naipes* could have come from the Flemish word *knaep*, for paper, for there was much trade between Flanders and Spain, and as card-making became an industry many countries exported cards.

Playing cards, as we have seen, were the subject of many

decrees; some protests against gambling, such as the decrees issued in Paris prohibiting play on working days, some like that of Henry VII of England, whose own daughter Margaret apparently shared the gambling fever with her father's subjects. He forbade servitors and apprentices to gamble at any time save during the Christmas holiday period – thus protecting the card-making industry.

Although the Tarot remained the everyday cards, for the stencilled packs, although cheap and flimsy, were well within the reach of the working classes, famous artists and goldsmiths were commissioned to design more elaborate packs for rich private patrons, as we have seen with the Visconti pack, and this practice continued up to the days of the French Revolution. Indeed, there were playing cards of silver at the court of Louis XV of France. After the stencil, came the wood block printing thought to have arrived in Germany with the coming of traders who had travelled to Russia from China by way of Arabia. The very first wood engravings may well have been playing cards, for the earliest known examples in existence are the 'Little Saints', illustrations of saints and ecclesiastical subjects printed in the monasteries, but which could have been adapted from the dimensions and techniques used by the earliest German card-makers. This new process made cards cheaper, more durable and more easily available to the public.

The decree by Edward IV forbidding the import of foreign cards into England shows the extent of their popularity and the rapidity of the growth of the card-making industry. Although most countries manufactured cards, France remained the greatest exporter. Bordeaux, for instance, made cards expressly for the Spanish market, called *Hombre* packs, and other centres in France exported cards to England, Holland, Bavaria, Germany and South America, all fashioned to suit the tastes and attitudes of each country.

The English cards of the Tudor period, sometimes made in France, and called 'decks' of cards or sometimes 'paires', mirrored the fashions at court. In Henry VII's time they showed the ladies with the lappets over their ears, and the knaves with their flat caps and red, yellow and green stockings, while later cards, in Elizabeth's reign, depicted the

Queens with the crowns perched perilously on the back of their heads.

A century before the first wood engravings a French knight, Etiene Vignoles, created a new pack and a new game called Piquet. This game was based on the rules of chivalry, and used only thirty-eight cards, dropping all the threes, fours and fives, the Page and the trumps of the Tarot. The suit signs were changed to Cups for the Church, Carreaux or arrowheads for the archers or vassals, Trèfles or clover for the farmer and piques or the point of the lance for the knights. The court cards were often named for famous knights such as Lancelot or kings such as Alexander. From these innovations come our modern suit emblems of cups, diamonds, clubs and spades. Some authorities think the suit of Carreaux, our diamonds, symbolized the tiles on the floors of the merchants' exchanges and represented the mediaeval guilds, rather than the archers and their arrowheads. Our suit of spades, the 'Piques' of Piquet, are named for the Spanish *espadas* or swords, and our diamonds may have been influenced more by the Spanish money suit than by the Carreaux in Piquet.

So there were two kinds of packs used concurrently, the Tarot and the Piquet pack, and each, as the industry grew, became more elaborate and the designs and decorations more diversified. With the advent of printing, the working man also could afford to pick and choose from patience packs, fortune-telling packs, Piquet packs, and even Tarots had many kinds of different trumps, even though the older traditional Tarot still remained a firm favourite, particularly in the southern districts of France.

Educational card games were invented, the earliest being the work of a teaching Franciscan monk, Thomas Murner, in Switzerland at the beginning of the sixteenth century, as an aid to teaching philosophy. One famous pack was devised by Cardinal Mazarin for young King Louis XIV, and executed by a member of the French Academy, and included such subjects as geography, history, kings and queens of France, Greek mythology and a charming set illustrated with some of Aesop's fables. The earliest spiritual card game was invented by a Carmelite Father, Joseph of Antwerp in 1666, and was illustrated with incidents from biblical tales and texts. Later, with the Pope's approval, a Cloister series was published, made expressly for ecclesiastical and monastic orders on much the same lines. Early children's games ranged from alphabetical sets to games teaching military science. There were also books published, like *Le Passetemps de la Fortune* in 1634, giving instructions for foretelling with dice, interpretations of dreams and methods of divination with playing cards.

Famous artists and goldsmiths were commissioned in every European capital to produce appealing packs of cards as gambling became the pastime of the wealthy. In Britain, a gaming master was added to the list of tutors necessary to educate well born young ladies and gentlemen in the social graces, books were printed giving rules and procedures of gaming, and the first history of playing cards was published in 1704.

French and German court cards featured reigning monarchs as well as court dandies. English cards depicted the Gunpowder Plot, the Horrid Popish Plot, the Spanish Armada, John Gay's *Beggars' Opera*, and even commemorated the South Sea Bubble scandal; while some Dutch packs also satirized the Bubble Disaster and political subjects. Viennese cards included a set of Tarots with the trumps depicting famous stage personalities. Anything and everything became the subject of the trumps, from animal Tarots to famous ballerinas and different dances and operettas, and later cards even illustrated characters from the novels of Sir Walter Scott.

However, when Napoleon came to power, he relegated all the court cards to waste paper baskets and commissioned such famous neo-classicists as the artist and sculptor David to design new packs of cards depicting worthy but rather dull subjects such as revolutionary heroes, gods and goddesses of ancient Greece and Rome (with Napoleon himself as Caesar!). There was naturally a later series featuring the French front line regiments and all the great French victories against the English. Not surprisingly, a later English set commemorated Wellington's victories against the French. But this new fashion was not popular, and after Napoleon's final defeat, the cardmakers, many of whom had gone out of business, resumed making their fanciful cards and the only innovation which did not lose its appeal was the fortune-telling pack of Marie le Normand, and of course the many books published during the Napoleonic period on the popular methods of divination. There had been a pack of divinatory cards issued to commemorate Napolean's return, which soon went out of existence.

There were Tarot cards made in England reflecting the craze for chinoiserie that swept through the Regency period while Holland produced beautiful patience packs with oriental subjects and heraldic cards came from every country. The Joker was introduced in America in the middle of the nineteenth century for the new game of euchre and the later American packs featured subjects such as cartoon comic characters, army and navy series and even a pack depicting bicycles of every kind. One featured the methods of cooking meat and other dishes, and was in fact an early cookery book. As late as 1915, there was a satirical pack of cards made in Australia with a wartime patriotic flavour, with caricatures of the reigning British monarch and national leaders as the trumps. In spite of all the interesting subjects, beautiful designs, witty verses and clever presentations, these beautifully designed cards never succeeded in equalling the powerful appeal of the original fourteenth century. Tarots, which remain today, after six hundred years, mysterious and fascinating.

The Major Arcana:
Its Symbology and Meanings

The Tarot Pack consists of seventy-eight cards in all. The twenty-two picture cards are called the Major Arcana, or the trumps of 'triumphs'. The fifty-six suit cards are divided into four suits and are called the Minor Arcana. The Major Arcana are numbered to twenty-one. The Fool or Jester is usually unnumbered, although some packs number this card 'O', and some Tarot packs place it at the end, rather than at the beginning of the sequence. But this does not matter for the purpose of divination.

CARD NUMBER ONE

THE MAGICIAN,
MAGUS OR PAGAD

Origin

This card is sometimes known as the Magus, after the leader of the Mithraic community whose task it was to introduce candidates into the mysteries and into the presence of the gods. He is linked with Mercury, guide to the souls in the underworld, and messenger of the gods. Mercury was gifted with divination, but was known as something of a super salesman, a sharp operator with 'the gift of the gab'. The word mercator, to sell, comes from him, and words were peculiarly his own property, for he was renowned for his propensity for disseminating news and gossip. He loved anything new, particularly ideas, and ruling as he did all kinds of mental dexterity, it is not surprising that quick thinking, guile, cunning and trickery became associated with Hermes or Mercury. The eternal mischief maker, his later prototypes were Harlequin, Puck, the Elfin Cobbler, the Little Red Sprite of Florence and Robin Goodfellow of England. Often he is depicted in Italian packs as a cobbler and is known as *Il Bagattel* or *Bagatto*; this word derives from *Bagatt*, meaning gossip, and is the derivation of another name for this card, THE PAGAD.

Description

This card shows a young man dressed as either a cobbler or a magician. If depicted as a cobbler, he wears multicoloured garments and a large brimmed hat, shaped a little like a figure eight lying on its side. He holds a small rod or tool in his left hand, and stands behind a table on which lie various tools of the cobbler's trade. The figure eight shape is said by some scholars to represent the Cosmic Lemniscate, a figure considered by ancient Egyptians to be the symbol of eternal life, and the rod is possibly derived from the Caduceus, the traditional staff of Mercury. As a magician, he wears a white robe, blue sash and red cloak. He holds a wand high in his right hand, and points his left hand to the earth. Above his head is the figure eight shape, the *lemniscate*, which other scholars consider derived from headwear similar to that of Mercury, which was often portrayed on the earliest Tarot cards. At his feet are lilies and roses.

Symbolic Meaning

This first card has a dual meaning which some packs of cards point up by depicting the magician's girdle as a serpent holding its tail in its mouth. This is the occult symbol for knowledge and duality. On the highest level, it symbolizes the seeker of spiritual truth, the union of the personal and the divine, power, subtlety and diplomacy; but on the other level it symbolizes the use and abuse of occult power for selfish ends, domination, deceit, trickery, devious methods and lies.

Actual Meaning

The Commencement card: initiative, will, self awareness, the ability to translate thought into action, willingness to take risks resulting in triumph, the guidance of occult forces, learning, new skills, new facts, new careers.

Reversed Meaning

Delay, uncertainty, guile, trickery, misuse of occult powers.

Combinations

When this card is placed near THE DEVIL or THE WHEEL, it has the effect of delaying events or causing hesitation. If placed next to DEATH, it cancels itself out.

THE HIGH PRIESTESS
OR PAPESSA

Origin

LA PAPESSA

Juno, sister of the earth mother and also her alter ego, Hera the mistress. The pomegranate often displayed in early cards shows the link with Persephone, queen of the dead, known as Juno Inferna, Juno's dark aspect. When taken to Italy she became Iana, and Juno, Diana and Iana all come from the root *div* meaning to shine. She symbolized the moon. When the Egyptian culture was absorbed by the Romans, she was equated with Isis and carried the assurance of life after death. In many fourteenth century manuscripts, Luna was depicted as an abbess which was also a popular idea in Celtic mythology, where both Brigid, the Celtic queen of heaven and Morrigan (Morgan le Fay's derivation) who was the counterpart of Persephone were portrayed in ecclesiastical garb. The Pope Joan legend, adapted from an earlier legend by a thirteenth century Dominican monk, derives from a legend of Juno. Juno was often used to invoke memory in ancient talismans which gave oracular and prophetic power to the wearer. The HIGH PRIESTESS title came from the revival of classical interest in the eighteenth century and refers to the role of the priestess who acted the part of the goddess during the Greek mysteries.

Description

A seated female figure, crowned or wearing a crescent moon head dress, holds a partly unrolled scroll which is half hidden by her garments. She wears a solar or ansated cross at her breast. In some packs she sits in between two pillars, one black, one white, which some occultists claim represent the Pillars of Boaz and Jakin, the negative and positive elements. The palm leaves and pomegranates often depicted in this card are said to represent the masculine and the feminine elements of creativity. Other cards picture her with a crescent moon at her feet and wearing a horned head dress, symbolizing Isis, the goddess of the moon. The book is thought to be the Tora or divine law by some authorities, and these cards often have the letters T.O.R.A. depicted on the scroll.

Symbolic Meaning

As contrasted with THE MAGICIAN, she is passive, the female element representing spiritual enlightenment and the inner life. She stands for esoteric truths, hidden knowledge, mystery, silence, the unrevealed future, hidden influences, philosophy and learning.

Actual Meaning

This card stands for occult studies, creative talent, divination, mysticism, esoteric knowledge and a thirst for learning. It brings satisfaction from studies, can often denote the teacher, means hidden things revealed, safety and spiritual protection, duality, mystery and cultural advancement.

Reversed Meaning

Sensuous pleasure, mere surface learning, other things delayed but not weakened.

Combinations

If placed next to THE WHEEL and both cards are upright it adds strength and balance to the latter and means a certain recompense in a law suit or petition which could seem hopeless at the outset. When reversed, in the same position, this meant a blighted future, loss of stability and a violent upheaval. If reversed and followed by an upright TEMPERANCE, it means that future prospects are very dark, for this combination brings almost unconquerable obstacles, bewilderment and the inability to act or to find a solution.

35

CARD NUMBER THREE

THE EMPRESS

Origin

The Earth Mother, Demeter, Eleusis, Vesta or Bona Dea. The mother of Dionysus, himself the central figure in the Greek mysteries. She shares with other traditions, the death of her son brought about by his enemies, the loss, the unobtainable quest for life and happiness, and the joy after mourning, when her son is reborn as a new entity. She represents fruitfulness, gestation, nourishment and is nature abundant.

Description

Seated on a throne she holds a sceptre in her left hand, in some cards ornamented with a crux ansata, others a cross surmounted by a ball. On her right there sits a shield, decorated with an eagle or a cross. She wears a crown or a diadem on her long abundant hair, and in some cards, she is depicted wearing a necklace of pearls and flowing robes that hint at coming motherhood. Often she is seen with trees behind her, corn waving around her, and water at her feet.

Symbolic Meaning

The productive vivifying life principle, the seed-to-flower process, fertility and fecundity. As opposed to logical intellect she symbolizes spiritual feeling and intuitive emotion. She also stands for progeny and growth, harmony in nature. To the artist, she brings inspiration and energy necessary for creative endeavour, and to the farmer she brings growth and abundance. To the lover she brings marriage, often a wealthy

36

union, and children.

Actual Meaning
A strong force, a natural course of events which proves beneficial, domestic stability and harmony, the good life. She brings material wealth and marriage, often wealthy; a kind benefactor, she brings good health after illness. She also symbolizes mother love, children, artistic creation, land tillage and abundance.

Reversed Meaning
Luxury loving laziness, maternal tyranny, domestic upheaval, war or destruction, wasting of talents or resources. An inevitable event will be slightly delayed.

Combinations
When this card precedes THE MAGICIAN, diplomacy brings the means of success. If this card precedes THE CHARIOT there will be a decisive victory in the material sense. If this card is reversed in the same position, the victory will be delayed but inevitable.

CARD NUMBER FOUR

THE EMPEROR

Origin

This image traces back to the horned gods, and is associated with Priapus. It is possibly directly conceived from an ancient talisman found in the Arab *Grimoire* and *The Picatrix*, the sacred book of esoteric magic, which shows a crowned king, sitting on a throne, a globe beneath his feet and a raven on his bent forearm. It was believed that this talisman brought the wearer great power, potency and honours. Some mediaeval artists are thought to have incorporated Charlemagne himself into this design, as Byzantian influence shown in the dress of this card and its female counterpart THE EMPRESS, in some of the earlier Tarot packs.

Description

A crowned masculine kingly figure is seated on a throne which is decorated sometimes with rams' heads, the symbol of Mars, or a lion's head (the symbol of Leo and the sun). He holds a sceptre in his right hand, sometimes decorated with a crux ansata, the symbol of eternal life, and a shield sits at his right side, featuring either an eagle or a cross. Sometimes he is depicted with a beard, a symbol of wisdom and endurance. Some packs show him with feet planted firmly on land while mountains rise in the distance, representing terrestrial domination and unyielding power.

Symbolic Meaning

As contrasted with THE EMPRESS, whose domination is of

hearth and home, and the forces of nature, THE EMPEROR is the dominating male force. He stands for rule of the masses, governorship, temporal power, logic, analysis, intellectual ability and willpower.

Actual Meaning
Wealth and power of the temporal kind, leadership, stability, creative energy, mental activity, knowledge through experience, intelligence dominating passion.

Reversed Meaning
The passions triumph over the intelligence, justice, possibly pity and mercy shown, clemency, loss of wealth, emotional immaturity, weakening of power.

Combinations
When coming in front of THE WORLD, and if upright, this means a lull in war, a state of truce, or a transient peace. If reversed, this means war on a national scale, conflict for the individual and loss of power of position on a world scale.

THE POPE OR HIEROPHANT

Origin

Jupiter, the all-forgiving father to whom the guilty turned for forgiveness, through the intercession of the priests. A similar talisman in *The Picatrix* in Babylonian times showed the crowned figure seated on what the Quabalists called the Merkebah Throne, sometimes depicted as a chariot, surrounded by the four Holy Living Creatures referred to in Ezekiel. It was thought to give the wearer or possessor the key to hidden knowledge, spiritual healing and regeneration, also inspiration and genius.

Description

Mediaeval artists often depicted him as the Pope or a monk, but the fourteenth century Visconti pack shows the god Jupiter, while the Florentine Minchiate pack depicts the Pope carrying a globe surmounted by an eagle. He sits between two pillars wearing the pontiff's crown and carries a sceptre or a triple cross in his left hand, while his right hand is lifted in the sign of benediction. He sometimes wears a Maltese cross or wears gloves and slippers embroidered with them. Some packs feature the crossed keys, the symbols of hidden doctrine and authority. In front of him kneel penitents, or priests. The two pillars, a recurring theme of the Tarot, are said by some scholars to represent the pull in opposite directions, the freedom of choice of the individual of the straight and narrow or the broad path.

Symbolic Meaning

In contrast with the preceding card of temporal rule, and with the PAPESSA or HIGH PRIESTESS who denotes hidden esoteric knowledge, this card stands for spiritual domination and traditional teachings for the masses. He rules over the externals of religion and his teaching is both practical and oral.

Actual Meaning

Preference for ritual, the established forms of religion and teachings, conventional adherence to established forms, desire for social approval, secrets revealed, scientific or religious vocation. This is the inspirational card of genius, particularly for those connected with the performing arts.

Reversed Meaning

Gullibility, delayed ambitions, unconventionality, a late vocation, adoption of modern ideas and innovations, craft, guile and distortion of truth, and treachery.

Combinations

When THE EMPEROR and THE HIEROPHANT come together it means a struggle within the enquirer's soul between materialistic and spiritual desires. The outcome will depend upon which card comes first. If both cards are reversed, and THE HIEROPHANT preceding THE EMPEROR, wealth will be lost through pride and failure through lack of knowledge will be possible. If the other way round, this wealth and power will be lost through the abandonment of skills or through lack of learning.

CARD NUMBER SIX

THE LOVERS

Origin

The origin of this card explains the rather bewildering additional meanings of trial and choice attributed to it. It originally depicted the Judgement of Paris, when Eros, the mischievous son of the goddess Aphrodite, so blinded the eyes of Paris with love that in choosing the fairest of Hera, Athena and Aphrodite, he gave the golden apple to the latter and incurred the wrath and enmity of the other two goddesses. The earlier card portrayed all three goddesses, but the later ones only two, with Eros hovering above with his quiver full of arrows tipped with gold and lead. The gold-tipped arrows were the shafts of love, and the leaden-tipped the stings of disillusion. A popular Venus or love talisman in *The Picatrix* showed a naked maiden wreathed in myrtle and roses, holding a mirror, and tethered by a golden chain to a handsome young man who stood beside her stroking her long flowing hair. Above them, of course, floated a plump little boy with his bow and arrow. This talisman, fashioned when Venus was ascending the first ten degrees of Taurus, Pisces or Leo, was said to bring beauty, happiness and love.

Description

There have been many changes in the form of this card since De Gébelin depicted it as married life, and Papus followed it with a picture of domestic felicity in the form of a family of mother, father and son, but in the earlier Florentine decks, Paris himself is shown kneeling at the feet of the goddesses, sometimes holding the golden apple, sometimes without it.

42

The more modern decks portray either two women, disparate often in either age or dress, or a youth standing between two women who seem to portray vice and virtue, or simply two lovers hand in hand, with mischievous Cupid hovering overhead in the act of releasing the arrow. He is usually nestling on a fleecy cloud or portrayed in a sunburst, looking rather amused at the predicament of the young man who seems to have a difficult choice. Waite's LOVERS trump shows the Rosicrucian influence, for he has an angel apparently uniting a couple; the man, standing in front of the Tree of Life, has only eyes for the woman, but the woman, standing in front of the Tree of Knowledge, looks at the angel for guidance.

Symbolic Meaning

The weighing up of future actions in the light of vice and virtue or positive and negative. The duality of the individual, the freedom of choice; the twin forces of good and evil; the two kinds of love, sacred and profane. The harmony of inner and outer existence.

Actual Meaning

Emotional trial resulting in success, choice, love and marriage after choice; trial, moral choice depending upon integrity of client, choice between sacred and profane love; harmony, beauty, attraction, idealistic friendship, vaccillation, instability, hesitation; flash of insight which suddenly solves a problem.

Reversed meaning

Quarrels and partings, the breaking of engagement or marriage, a moral lapse, the wrong choice, wanting the best of both worlds, outside interference, possibly parental, quarrels over offspring.

Combinations

THE LOVERS, coming in front of THE CHARIOT, brings revelation of betrayal. If THE CHARIOT comes first, then this means that a sudden departure will put paid to a venture or a romance. If THE LOVERS precedes THE MAGICIAN there will be indecision in commencing a new artistic venture, while if THE LOVERS is reversed in front of THE MAGICIAN this will mean a separation due to indecision and hesitation.

CARD NUMBER SEVEN

THE CHARIOT

Origin

Zeus, Aries or Mars, son of Jupiter the All-Father. Contrasted with THE POPE who means divine stability, this card represents the symbol of divine destruction, as also did Thor in Scandinavian mythology, Balor in Irish mythology and Sekhmet in Egyptian. A talisman, very similar to this symbol, fashioned when Mars ascended the first ten degrees of Scorpio, was said by *The Picatrix* to give a man courage and honour in war and success in competitive activities. It featured a canopied chariot drawn by lions. Mediaeval artists often portrayed Mars standing in a chariot, sometimes brandishing a sword or a whip, and sometimes with a halberd. Winged horses often drew the chariot.

Description

The fifteenth century cards often depicted Mars brandishing a sword, while the cards attributed to Gringonneur in 1392 show Mars wielding a mighty battleaxe. De Gébelin considered this card Osiris triumphant, or the conquering sun.

The charioteer wears a crown and carries a sceptre denoting victory and triumph. On his shoulders, like epaulettes, lie two faces, thought to represent rule over two opposing forces, while the animals depicted drawing the chariot are sometimes lions, sometimes horses, sometimes a black and white sphinx. These are said to represent the carnal and spiritual forces over which the charioteer has firm control. The four pillars

44

in each corner, upholding the canopy of the chariot, are said to represent the four cardinal elements fire, air, earth, and water. On some cards water, mountains and castles can be seen in the background, and laurel leaves or wreaths and winged suns are often found decorating the front of the chariot.

Symbolic Meaning
Man conquering on the lower plane, controlling his own nature and mastering the animal passions. The combination of material and physical powers, the union of positive and negative. The triumph of balanced forces, with justice tempered with mercy.

Actual Meaning
The card of greatness, not inherited success but success through personal effort. Success for those engaged in artistic pursuits. Triumph over all kinds of difficulties, and health. Achievement, wealth and honour. Speedy travel in luxurious conditions. Unexpected news by word of mouth; the routing of enemies.

Reversed Meaning
Warning to conquer the animal passions. Victory through evil methods, unfortunate news or the collapse of plans, the defeat of ambition, ruthlessness, egocentricity.

Combinations
If this card is followed by THE MOON, it means that news will come to light that has been kept secret for a long time. If THE CHARIOT follows THE MOON, there will be illness, and if THE MOON is reversed, the danger, illness or scandal will not be so strong.

JUSTICE OR
THE BALANCE

Origin

Perhaps symbolizing one of the four cardinal virtues or moral precepts of the ancient Greek Stoic philosophers, the first of which, JUSTICE, was always depicted as a female. This figure could derive from Themis, who married Zeus and bore Astraea, now our modern constellation Virgo, or could perhaps derive from Athena, goddess of war, whom the Romans called Minerva. She stood, as well as for the more subtle tactics of warfare, for all things pertaining to the mind, for wisdom, vigilance and dispassionate justice. Some of the older cards seem closer to this concept for they depict Justice brandishing a sword, just as Athena brandished her thunderbolt.

Description

In some packs, Justice is seen as an angel or a winged figure; in others she is shown sitting on a throne between the customary two pillars between which is stretched a curtain or veil. In one set of cards, she wears a turreted crown, in others a double crown but in all she carries a double-edged sword upraised, in her right hand, at her left, a set of scales or balances. In some packs, there is grass at her feet. She is not blindfolded, as she represents Justice in the all-seeing spiritual sense. In ancient Egyptian belief it was thought that the god Thoth supervised the weighing of the souls of the dead in the Great Balance, on which it was recorded if the heart balanced the symbol of righteousness which was a feather. If it did so, then the soul won its immortality and joined the gods in everlasting life.

Symbolic Meaning
Successful combinations, balanced judgement. Modern methods in education replacing outworn creeds. Control. Justice is served.

Actual Meaning
Equity, balance, balanced arbitration, the voice of inner conscience, trial and rehabilitation, honesty, justice, good outcome of legal and educational concerns. Good combination of materials, a well balanced outlook, vindication of truth and integrity depending upon the moral position of client.

Reversed Meaning
Bigotry, injustice, unjust condemnation, legal tangles, severity, overharsh judgement used against a fellow man.

Combinations
When preceding THE HIGH PRIESTESS, this card means secrets come to light connected with the law. If following, it has much the same meaning, but the facts will have only come to light through legal matters. If both are inverted then events connected with the law or justice will miscarry.

CARD NUMBER NINE

THE HERMIT

Origin

Saturn, or as he was known in Greece, Kronos, is the origin of this card. The two names became confused with the Roman god Chronus, the god of time. The idea of time became associated with Saturn because longevity, age, slow cautious progress are all connected with this god. Saturn, after years of parental oppression, castrated his own father with an iron sickle, and later devoured his offspring, but was eventually tricked and overpowered by his own son Zeus. The sickle is the derivation of the scythe or reaping hook associated with Old Father Time and with death, and the hour glass with Chronus. Because the element of dark oppression was connected with Saturn early astrologers had little that was cheerful to say about this planet, but instead of gloom and restriction, modern astrologers consider him to be a benevolent taskmaster, who hides a warm heart beneath a cold exterior. Other associations with Saturn seem to be love of learning and cunning, the completion of a cycle of life, wisdom or a great lesson to be learned. Talismans for longevity and wisdom show an old man with an hour glass in hand, often accompanied by a stag, which was another symbol for long life.

Description

The early Mantegna decks gave him the title Cronico, and some pictured him as a hermit with an indistinguishable animal at his side. On others he was portrayed as Old Father

48

Time with all the instruments of chronology beside him, while others showed him as a beggar or friar carrying and leaning on a staff. The hour glass has now been replaced by a lantern, giving rise to the name 'The Light of the World' bestowed upon this card by early moralists. Levi insisted that this card meant prudence, the hermit travelling the *via prudentia* throughout life, but this was his substitution purely made to fit his sequence of moral progression for a system which did not include a PRUDENCE among the trumps. A bearded old man, in cloak and sandals, carries a lantern before him as if feeling his way by its light. He leans heavily on his staff as he goes on his journeyings. Sometimes he is standing on grassy fields, sometimes mountains tower behind him.

Symbolic Meaning

He is an explorer or a venturer. A solitary, making his way carefully, with the help of his staff and by the light of his lantern. He is often bearded, his cloak the protection of wisdom, his staff his protection, and the light thought by some authorities to symbolize the light of occult science, his guide. He keeps straight on, letting no one deflect him, albeit slowly and deliberately, taking care that nothing will put out his light, strengthened by the gifts of the divine spirit in his search for wisdom and truth.

Actual Meaning

This card takes a lot of its meanings from the surrounding cards. It means no progress without thought or planning. It denotes wisdom from above; silent counsel; the voice of the inner self; a secret revealed; a slowing down of things; deliberation and prudence needed. A beneficial meeting with a wise person. A prospective journey. Attainment after delay.

Reversed Meaning

Irksome delays or failure through fear of the unknown, excess fear and caution. Deceit. Stubbornness impeding progress.

Combinations

If this card is followed by THE HIGH PRIESTESS, this seems a secret will never be revealed. If THE HIGH PRIESTESS follows THE HERMIT then the secret after patient endeavour will be discovered. If both are inverted this means delay, but revelations nevertheless. If THE HERMIT comes together with THE DEVIL, these two cards influence all the other cards around them. If THE DEVIL precedes THE HERMIT then his power will prevail, but if the other way around, THE HERMIT will shine light on underhand methods and powerful enemies so that good will prevail. If THE DEVIL is inverted, the process will be delayed but eventually right will triumph.

THE WHEEL OF
FORTUNE

Origin

The words fate and prudence have relevance to the origin and derived meanings of this card. Fate, the word from which we obtained fairy, is linked with the Moirae, the triple goddesses of ancient Greece, those three spinners who held the threads of men's destinies in their hands. They gave rise to countless legends of the fairy spinners, and in Saxon times were known as the three Wyrds and as such were the inspiration for Shakespeare's weird sisters. An ancient talisman for the strengthening of the memory and the bestowal of prudence was the symbol of Janus, the Roman god of doorways who had one head looking into the future and the other looking back at the past. Another such image used was of Cerberus, the infernal hound, who had three heads, ruling past, present and future. This seems to have been the basis for THE WHEEL OF FORTUNE portrayed on the Marseilles pack, for they show either the head of a wolf or an old man on the left of the wheel, denoting memory or the past, a lion or mature man in the centre, denoting intelligence or the present, and the head of a dog or a youth on the right of the wheel, standing for foresight or the future. Some later talismans giving prudence, showed a female figure holding a spiked wheel. The wheel on this trump possibly derives from Ixion, who after being caught in dalliance with the wife of Zeus, was bound to a fiery wheel to spin throughout all eternity. A popular concept of Satan in mediaeval times was a wheel hung with the souls of the damned and rotated with evident relish by Satan.

Description

Some early packs took the legend of King Midas who was awarded ass's ears by Apollo, after having given the judgement of a musical contest in favour of Pan, for their mode of THE WHEEL OF FORTUNE. Four ass-eared figures are rotating around the wheel, with the inscriptions, 'I will rule. I have ruled. I am without rule. I rule.' Many Egyptian symbols were inserted during the reconstruction of the cards by such authorities as de Gébelin, Etteilla, Wirth and Waite, possibly because the wheel was used in Egyptian temples to denote the brevity of all human endeavour and the inconstancy of fortune. In some cards the wheel is set between two pillars, resting on leaves. A winged and crowned figure sitting at the top holding a cornucopia or horn of plenty, is menaced by a stealthy jackal or a fox. In others the Egyptian god Osiris sits at the top, or sometimes a sphinx, while on the rim the jackal-headed Anubis sits opposite Set, the Evil One, who is portrayed as a wolf. In other cards are found the four Holy Living Creatures found in Ezekiel, the lion, the eagle, the bull and Aquarius or man. Sometimes a serpent is found at the top of the wheel and the letters T.A.R.O. lettered around the hub interspersed with the signs for mercury, sulphur, salt and water to correlate with the astrological symbols of the four holy figures.

Symbolic Meaning

Liberation from the round of incarnation, the gaining of wisdom and balance. The eternal process of evolution. The capriciousness of fate, the law of retribution of Karma, the unexpected twist of affairs that turns everything upside down.

Actual Meaning

'As ye sow so shall ye reap'. A new cycle in affairs. The solving of a problem through the progression of events. Destiny, success, good fortune, unexpected beneficial change, a reward of material wealth through past efforts.

Reversed Meaning

A slower and more difficult change, depending upon surrounding cards for rewards being fortunate or the opposite.

Combinations

If close to THE MAGICIAN, THE HERMIT, THE WORLD, or THE HIGH PRIESTESS, this is a very fortunate sign, and with THE CHARIOT this card means a great triumph. If followed by THE MAGICIAN a happy and exciting change of profession, dwelling or direction in life. If THE MAGICIAN comes first the change will occur but later, and will bring success gradually. If THE HERMIT is near THE WHEEL this means light will be shed on hidden factors bringing success. THE WHEEL, when followed by THE HIGH PRIESTESS, means an artistic or scientific triumph, but if this order is reversed, the client has gifts he has not been able to develop, but through a new twist of fate will be able to do so, leading to great satisfaction and achievement.

CARD NUMBER ELEVEN

FORTITUDE: STRENGTH
OR THE ENCHANTRESS

Origin

The origin of this figure is thought to be Cyrene. She was the handmaiden of Artemis, the moon goddess, who was seen by the Sun one day when she was wrestling barehanded with a lion. He became enamoured, and after obtaining the advice of a wise centaur he carried her off, mated with her and the result was a son, Aristaeus the huntsman god. Talismans using figures like that of FORTITUDE were used to bind men to beasts, for ancient occultists believed that certain people possessed magical powers over the animal kingdom. The lion, the symbol of the sun or the masculine principle, was often coupled in magical lore with the unicorn, that fabled animal symbol of virginity and the moon.

Description

The early Minchiate packs showed a female Samson-like figure breaking a Grecian column in two with apparent ease. Others depicted a man clubbing a lion to death, this perhaps deriving from the legend of the labours of Hercules and linked again with the sun.

A young woman, sometimes depicted wearing a hat, or with the cosmic lemniscate over her head, with no apparent effort and evincing no fear whatsoever, is either opening or closing the jaws of a rather sleepy looking lion. Sometimes she wears a crown instead of the hat and sometimes she wears roses in her hair and around her waist. The rose is said to symbolize the invincible union of desires and spiritual strength.

Symbolic Meaning

The moral force of purity which subdues passions and baser desires. The triumph of the spirit over the material world. The triumph of love over hate, of the positive forces over the negative, sacred love over profane.

Actual Meaning

Self discipline, strength and endurance, events overcome by willpower, moral victory, tolerance overcoming prejudice, mastery of circumstances, mastery of life, 'right is might'. Opportunity to put plans into action if the client has the courage to risk it. 'Stand fast, take courage'. The mind's domination over material adversities.

Reversed Meaning

There is no reversed meaning for FORTITUDE as this card dominates the other Major Arcana appearing with it and always remains the same. It is a very fortunate card indeed!

Combinations

This card is very strong and influences the whole of the layout. When followed by DEATH, it means an illness, serious but not fatal. When DEATH precedes FORTITUDE this means an abrupt and violent death; if both these cards are reversed, a narrow escape from injury and death. If FORTITUDE comes before THE CHARIOT, there will be a triumph after considerable effort. If THE CHARIOT comes first, this means great strength in future trials.

CARD NUMBER TWELVE

THE HANGED MAN

Origin

Thought to derive directly from the Orphic mystery rites and the worship of Dionysus, this card is said to depict sacrifice in order to achieve regeneration. This has a corollary in the stories of Jesus, Odin and Osiris. In ancient times many images of Dionysus were hung in trees to ensure fertility. The death of the old year in pagan Britain was symbolized by the stoning of an effigy of Jack o' Lent, or the Lord of Misrule. The Saturnalia and the Winter Carnival are derivatory of these beliefs. Mediaeval artists often depicted THE HANGED MAN as Judas Iscariot, bound or 'baffled' by the heels, which was the punishment meted out to criminals and debtors, and show the thirty pieces of silver falling from his pockets. The eighteenth-century occultists showed a semi-feminine youth posed erect, one foot loosely attached to a stake in the ground. The Rosicrucian school considered this card to mean the adept bound by his own engagements.

Description

The hanging figure seems peculiarly placid and at his ease, although suspended upside down, almost as if he is in a trance. He is suspended from his left foot on a rough gallows that is made from trees, and there are six branches either side. His arms form a triangle and his legs a cross. He is shown in some cards with only one shoe, and in some flowers bloom at the foot of the gibbet. Some cards depict him with a halo of light around his head, while others show coins falling from his pockets.

Symbolic Meaning

This card symbolizes a sacrifice, uncomplaining but entailing some suffering and hardship. It also means the complete reversal of a way of life; the changing of the natural order by a strong spiritual force. The falling coins are thought to portray a contempt for worldly riches.

Actual Meaning

Spiritual decision bringing serenity, wisdom, initiation, divination, intuition, suspended decisions, self-sacrifice, the gaining of inward peace and wisdom, occult prophetic power. Not always a happy card, for depending upon the surrounding cards, it can denote renunciation, destruction and abandonment.

Reversed Meaning

Vague idealism, futile sacrifice, selfishness, self absorption, hypocrisy, hidden plans, love of material things, false prophecy, arrogance, dependence upon the physical world: sometimes it can denote a violent death.

Combinations

THE HANGED MAN and TEMPERANCE together mean hypocrisy of false promises bringing indecision. THE HANGED MAN and DEATH always mean a violent or unhappy demise or a matter involving sacrifice. If THE HANGED MAN precedes THE DEVIL, a great sacrifice will bring strength and power. THE DEVIL following THE HANGED MAN often refers to a combination, a partnership or marriage and shows that one or both of the partners will have to be prepared to give more.

CARD NUMBER THIRTEEN

DEATH

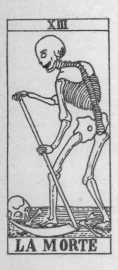

Origin

The origin of the card could be Moros, as the Greeks knew him. Mightier even than Zeus, he was the arbiter of Supreme Destiny. As did the Moire, he had three faces, Thanatos and Ked being the other two aspects, both pertaining to death. He is pictured here as the alter ego of Saturn, or time, waiting for no one, making no distinction between ruler and ruled. The original placement of this card was not number thirteen but was changed possibly because of the occult theory of numbers, based on the Qabbala. Most modern occultists, influenced by the probably Shamanic origin of the Tarot, now consider this card to mean not death but transformation or a stripping away of all the base metals to reveal the gold beneath.

Description

In some packs this card is shown as a skeleton reaping a harvest of heads, arms and bones. One pack shows heads of children and heads wearing crowns. Waite's pack portrays a solemn knight carrying a banner emblazoned with the rose of life. He is mounted upon a beautiful white horse, riding across a countryside upon which the sun beams from between two towers. In the distance mountains and water can be seen. In front of him, women and children fall powerlessly while a bishop eagerly awaits his coming, face radiant, hands outstretched in welcome.

Symbolic Meaning

A deeply spiritual card, meaning the casting off of the material and the transformation and regeneration of the soul. It does not mean death, necessarily, but can have a ruthless, sudden and almost shocking connotation of death of the old life and the rebirth of the soul. It stands for change, and can sometimes bring with it shock and destruction prior to rebirth. This sometimes means that the change is in the consciousness of the individual or can denote artistic work of some importance being created after a struggle, or a new way of life leading to creative activity.

Actual Meaning

This card, in older readings, used to mean the death of kings. It means the end of something prior to a change, destruction leading to transformation, change in consciousness. If badly aspected it can mean shocks and illness or all pretensions stripped away.

Reversed Meaning

Mortality, death or preoccupation with death. The lingering effects of death of a loved one. Wilful destiny. Stagnation and boredom. An enforced removal of something which should have been given up voluntarily.

Combinations

With THE FALLING TOWER, this means a national disaster. However, if THE FALLING TOWER is reversed, and DEATH upright then there will be narrow escapes from calamity. DEATH preceding THE WORLD means that a world leader will die or there will be a world-wide epidemic. DEATH followed by THE LOVERS, means the end of a marriage or a romance. When DEATH is inverted the marriage will be broken by death.

TEMPERANCE

Origin

This card may derive from Aquarius the Water Carrier, or perhaps Ganymede, the young prince of Troy who was abducted by Zeus to become the cupbearer of the gods and whose duty it was to refill the cup with the nectar of immortality whenever it became empty. The Egyptians always portrayed Aquarius with two vessels of water, and he, in turn, they identified with the god of the Nile, whose waters fed the lands in both a spiritual and a material sense. It has also been noted that mixing the water and wine was an ancient rite connected with Dionysus as his alter-ego Bacchus, and some Gnostic sects used two chalices to celebrate the Eucharist.

Description

In some packs this card is known as THE ANGEL OF TIME. It does not refer to temperance as we use it in the more modern sense, but more in a modifying, mitigating sense. It shows a winged angel or female figure in long flowing robes wearing either a solar sign or a flower on her forehead, pouring out liquid in a shining stream from a chalice in her right hand to a chalice in her left. One foot is placed upon the earth and one in the water in some packs. Usually mountain peaks are depicted in the distance. Some show a shining sun rising above these, and flowers and vegetation bloom at her feet.

Symbolic Meaning

The mountain peaks in the background are said to symbolize

wisdom and understanding, while the pouring of the liquid from one vessel into another is said to denote the descent of spirit into matter, or the purifying of the soul by spiritual grace. The liquid is thought to be the stuff of the mind, the spiritual food acting upon the materially minded to give inspiration. It is considered by others, coming after DEATH, the transformation card, to denote an oblation to the gods, the cleansing and strengthening of the new soul. It signifies the combination of active and passive forces, the unifying of the male and female elements, and the stream that is shown in one pack, in which an angel is standing, is said to represent the past, present and future.

Actual Meaning

Moderation, economy, successful combinations, adaptation, consolidation, concession towards a common goal, stalemate before synthesis. Success through good management, life, vitality, spiritual awareness and joy. It often means a rich marriage.

Reversed Meaning

This card annuls any vacillation or indecisiveness, ill-advised partnerships, clashing interests, clumsy handling of potential.

Combinations

TEMPERANCE preceding JUSTICE means a long legal process resulting in equity and justice. If JUSTICE comes first, there will be delays and the matter may not eventuate. However, when TEMPERANCE is inverted near this card, it puts an end to vacillation and hesitation. When with THE LOVERS this means indecision, hesitation, and deceit on the part of a lover.

CARD NUMBER FIFTEEN

THE DEVIL

Origin

The origin of this card is possibl[y] Saturn once again. A figure very similar to this mediaeval concept of Sata[n] was worshipped by the Knights Tem[plar] in a cult which appears to hav[e] been an off-shoot of Mithras, the Rom[an] warrior god, equated with Diony[sus], when the two cults blended toge[ther]. They worshipped the unconquer[ed] sun, whose birthday every year o[n] December 24th was celebrated by th[e] slaying of a bull whose blood wa[s] sprinkled over the soil, to defeat th[e] god of darkness. This links wit[h] Saturn, the death of winter and th[e] rebirth of the sun. The Bahomet o[r] Baphomet, a word derived from Ma[ho]hommed, simply meaning idol, wa[s] often carved to represent an old bearded man, sometime[s] with two or three faces, and glowing eyes. This was derive[d] from Janus, the guider of destinies and god of doorways an[d] beginnings. Sometimes these idols had a cat's head, sometime[s] horns or birds' claws, sometimes cloven hoofs, sometime[s] wings sprouting from the shoulders, and cords or serpent[s] binding the body. All these were connected with the worshi[p] of Satan. Christians thought this figure was Satan, and th[e] Templars were accused of Devil worship and black magic[.] Some modern packs still show the horns, the eagles' claws[,] the cloven hoofs and the cords or chains, while others portra[y] the figure wearing a shamanic helmet and bats' wings. Lev[i] changed the face of this card, for the earlier cards were no[t] particularly evil in aspect but more mischievous.

62

playing beneath the sun. In the Minchiate, the children have
become young lovers. Some early packs showed a spinner
spinning or unwinding thread. The Waite pack depicts a
joyous child astride a white horse, flourishing a large banner.
There are the ever familiar dew drops which de Gébelin
described as 'tears of pearl and gold'. In all cards the sun
beams down, rayed with light and dropping dew onto two
children who stand in front of a low stone wall. The children
are sometimes dancing, the sky is shining blue, there are sun-
flowers peeping over the wall and the card emanates a radiant
happiness and triumph.

Symbolic Meaning

This card symbolizes the end of self deception, the bright
warm light of day, innocence, purity, strength and courage,
the conquering regenerative force and positive thinking.

Actual Meaning

Triumph and achievement in any field, particularly in art and
science. Happy meetings, a wealthy marriage, liberation from
routine, gratitude for life's gifts, material happiness, the
realization of ambition, protection, studies completed, health,
joy and success against all odds, pleasure in simple things.

Reversed Meaning

This card, although weakened when reversed, still retains its
essential meaning.

Combinations

If this card precedes DEATH, there will be a triumph, through
something being finished, ending or dying. A death will bring
benefit or vindication. When with THE FALLING TOWER, out
of evil comes good, so a sudden catastrophe proves of ultimate
benefit.

CARD NUMBER TWENTY

JUDGEMENT

Origin

This card possibly has for its central figure St Michael, one of the seven Archangels who are said to be responsible for keeping the planets on their courses. Hermes and Michael have a function in common, for Michael guides the souls into the new world and Mercury was the guide to the souls in the underworld. This card has the connotation of reincarnation rather than the Christian concept of judgement for past sins and then rebirth.

Description

Some packs depict God among his angels. In the Etteilla pack there was no angel, and Papus conceived a rather sentimental card showing mother, father and child at the resurrection. Most later packs depict an angel blowing a trumpet from which hangs the cross of St Michael, over graves that are opening revealing naked figures with their arms stretched upwards. Sometimes the mountains are portrayed in the distance. Quite a number of older packs called this card THE ANGEL.

Symbolic Meaning

This card is the symbol of the eternal spirit, the cycle of birth in death, the end and the beginning of an existence, the Karmic round.

Actual Meaning

Resolution and completion. A mental awakening that could

precede fame and success. Justified pleasure in achievement. Change and renewal, a beneficial influence, a new lease of life, change of thought, a new philosophy, or a new way of life. The final outcome, a summing up.

Reversed Meaning
A highly spiritual card, this card loses its strength when surrounded by physical cards such as THE WHEEL OF FOR-TUNE, THE DEVIL or THE MAGICIAN. When reversed but not in company with any of these it means impermanent fame or transient success, loss of health or material possessions, bitterness or weakness, fear of death, or fear and bitterness in old age.

Combinations
This card is a very powerful card so when combined with THE CHARIOT it means fame and triumph. If reversed, the meaning is reversed too. If JUDGEMENT comes before THE CHARIOT reversed, it means the triumph will be short lived, for the effect of the sudden success will weaken the character. If THE HERMIT follows this card, triumph will always be of an inner spiritual kind, or will only be apparent after death. If THE HERMIT is reversed, there will be discoveries of great benefit made public.

CARD NUMBER TWENTY-ONE

THE WORLD

Origin

This trump is said to be derived directly from the Greek mysteries, and depicts the culmination of the rites, when the initiate, having successfully passed through his ordeals, is dressed in honour of the sun and presented to the populace. Indeed, Aupelius describes in detail his graduation at the conclusion of the rites, in *The Golden Ass*, and furnishes us with a description of the garments he wore. They consisted of a flower-embroidered robe and a long floating scarf called an olympian stole, while he carried a torch in one hand and a palm chaplet with leaves sticking out like the rays of the sun in the other. The early French packs titled this card THE CARD OF THE MAGI and it is not surprising that it is considered to be the best card in the pack, and carries the meaning of completion and reward.

Description

The old Visconti pack shows two cherubs supporting a globe containing towers that rise from the sea under the light of glittering stars. The picture is surrounded by a wreath or garland and in each corner are the familiar four living creatures found in Ezekiel, which also stood for the four cardinal elements and the four directions. In the more modern Tarots, a dancing female figure is shown, with left leg crossed behind her, a direct contrast to THE HANGING MAN. Sometimes she carries a mirror in her hand, or a rod, or two rods, one in both hands, and occasionally she is depicted holding a crown.

76

She is partially draped with a gracefully floating stole, and is pictured inside an oval Mandala or wreath, bound in four places by ribbon or roses. In each corner are the four living creatures.

Symbolic Meaning

The dancer denotes joy and happiness, the mirror derives from the Sistrum of Isis, the wreath and the crown denote joyous celebration and the attainment of the initiate who has mastered the truth. Levi says this garland, symbolizing truth, is less easily broken than chains of iron. It is the culmination of the entire series and represents finality, the final completion of the cycle which commenced with THE MAGICIAN, and led through triumphs, temptations, snares and new experiences, and entailed the casting off of the baser self, the discarding of false illusion and the finding of truth. It denotes the birth of a new being through the merging of consciousness with super-consciousness. This is the summing up, the reward for lessons well learned.

Actual Meaning

The seeker of perfection, the attainment of great success, material and spiritual. The occult, material or spiritual triumph, and reward. The lesson learned, individually perfected happiness, joy, celebration, movement, travel over water or across the world, a triumphant conclusion to a matter, or the end of a cycle.

Reversed Meaning

A person who is in a rut; the sacrifice of love for material considerations, fear of change, refusal to learn the lessons of life, over-attachment to possessions and surroundings, the fear of the unknown, failure of the will, stagnation.

Combinations

If this card is combined with THE SUN it brings a wonderful emotional experience, or joy, love and harmony. If it comes after THE HANGED MAN it denotes that a loving sacrifice will bring a triumph. If THE WORLD comes first, it means a sacrifice that could bring sadness and parting.

THE FOOL

Origin

IL MATTO

This card, sometimes at the beginning and sometimes at the end of the pack, is the derivation of our modern Joker and one of the most significant cards in the series. THE FOOL or THE JESTER as he is known is the direct descendant of the old 'Lord of Misrule' and of Dionysus himself. The amalgamation of Mithras and Dionysus brought with it a number of feasts and festive rites, the principal feasts of which were the Saturnalia. Only two remain today — Holy Innocents' day and Christmas Day. On Holy Innocents' day, the Lord of Misrule, or Dionysus in revolt, traditionally threw over the established rule and rebelled against the restrictions of authority as a symbol of his search for spiritual enlightenment and rebirth. His descendant THE FOOL, the eternal scapegoat, played an important part in mediaeval feudal society, and the motley and bells became an honoured and respected symbol of service. The jester's cap is thought to derive from the horns or asses' ears worn by Dionysus and early packs feature a type of horned jester's cap, and others show him clad in motley, and carrying a bladder and bells.

Description

He is portrayed in gay clothing, stepping out carelessly, sometimes with either a dog or a dragon snapping at his heels, a small bundle tied to the end of a stick across his shoulders. In some cards he carries a staff, in others he flourishes a white rose, and in most designs it appears he is just about to step off a precipice of which he seems unaware. Some early packs portrayed him as a penitential beggar clad in white, wandering the highways of life; others clad him in tattered rags.

Symbolic Meaning
Some authorities claim that the crocodile, considered by the Egyptians as the sacred and all-seeing, which is often portrayed at his heels denotes that THE FOOL is possessed of divine wisdom, and that he is ignoring the material world and commencing the journey of life, armed with a spiritual strength which will protect him from all physical dangers. He is the Eternal Traveller about to undergo any of the experiences of life in order to learn its secrets. He must make his choices, abandon, adopt, embrace or discard in order to attain perfection. Some early moralists, writing about this card, considered that the bundle or purse he carries contains all the sins and vices of the world.

Actual Meaning
A choice of vital importance needing great wisdom. 'Divine discontent'. The seeker of experiences, spiritually guided. The blithe spirit. Nevertheless, it also carries the elements of anarchy, the irrational human element, the unexpected, the breakdown of the existing order for the materialist, light-heartedness, heedlessness, recklessness and travel.

Reversed Meaning
A faulty choice or impediment to progress.

Combinations
This card being a highly spiritual card, it combines only with those on the same plane and is cancelled out by some powerful material cards such as THE WHEEL or THE DEVIL. If this card follows THE HERMIT a secret will come to light and be aired for discussion. If the other way around a secret is now safe. THE FOOL with THE CHARIOT denotes important news and THE FOOL and THE SUN mean something unexpected will occur that will bring order, comfort and happiness.

SOME GENERAL POINTS ON COMBINATIONS OF THE MAJOR ARCANA

Sometimes, when one strong card is inverted and precedes another strong card which is upright, one neutralizes the other. For instance THE EMPRESS and THE DEVIL; THE DEVIL and THE STAR; THE SUN and THE TOWER; all these cancel each other out.

JUSTICE which is a physical card, cannot combine with THE EMPRESS, nor does it combine well with THE WORLD, for THE WORLD is essentially an abstract card. THE HERMIT and THE WORLD are incompatible too, for THE HERMIT's symbology is too narrow to combine with that of THE WORLD. This also applies to THE MAGICIAN and THE WORLD. When JUSTICE comes before THE HANGED MAN it shows that clemency and tolerance should be shown rather than cold hard judgement. JUDGEMENT is a spiritual card, and concerned with intellectual matters, so it does not combine well with such physical cards as THE WHEEL OF FORTUNE or THE DEVIL. THE DEVIL is a card of events which must follow inexorably to a conclusion.

THE HIGH PRIESTESS gives self awareness and depth of meaning to all the other cards surrounding her, and often shows new avenues and opportunities for advancement.

FORCE is one of the strongest cards in the pack and sets the tone for the entire reading. It destroys THE STAR and even dominates THE DEVIL. Another card which influences every other card in the pack is THE TOWER. THE WORLD is the only card which can mitigate its influence, by making the outcome general rather than particular, as in a world scale misfortune such as an epidemic or a universal disaster. FORCE however would increase its potency and THE DEVIL its darker aspect.

Pairings and Trios

If there is a preponderance of the Major Arcana in the reading then destiny is taking a hand in the client's life and the events will be out of his control. If the cards seem to favour one suit, such as Wands, then the accent of the reading will be on career and business; if Cups, then love affairs and social life will predominate; if Pentacles, then money affairs would dominate the reading; and if Spades, the reading would contain much predicted turbulence, spiritual suffering and perhaps illness. If the court cards are all of the same suit the same emphasis would apply only more strongly, so that if all the court cards were of the Spades suit, the client would have a difficult time through envious and hostile enemies actively attacking him.

Pairs and three of a kind also have added meaning, very similar to those given when the ordinary playing cards are used for divination. For instance, three Jacks in an ordinary pack can mean workmen around the house, or conviviality. But sometimes three – and more particularly four – Jacks mean legal courts, police, scandal or prison. My first book, *Fortune-Telling*, gives all the meanings of the ordinary playing-cards in detail.

The Minor Arcana:
Its Symbology and Meanings

There are four suits in the Minor Arcana: Swords, Cups,
Pentacles, (they can be called Deniers) and Clubs which are
also known as Staves or Wands in some packs. They were
adapted by the French knight, de Vignoles (known as Lanire)
in the fifteenth century for the game of Piquet – a game of
chivalry – and his playing cards had carreaux or arrowheads, trefoils or flower cups and piques, the points of the
lances. (These may, alternatively, have meant square paving-
stones.) From these come our modern packs, the Cups being
our Hearts, the Carreaux or arrow heads our Diamonds, the
Trefoils of clovers our Clubs and the Piquet or lance points,
our Spades. The Tarot court, or 'coat' cards as they were first
known, include a Knave or Servitor as well as the Knight
(our Jack) and the King and Queen. Often in the early cards
the servitor or knave was depicted as a maid of honour, (the
name 'knave' simply meant 'son') and these cards can mean
either sex. Possibly the entourage was the representation of
a feudal court or mediaeval family.

The suit of Swords covers all things connected with spiritual stress, struggle, strife, battle, loss and worry, trials,
competition, and always loneliness of spirit. The suit of Cups
pertains to all things connected with love, joyous fulfilment,
procreation, home, success, friendship and human relation-
ships. The suit of Clubs rules all things concerned with the
lasting values, such as serenity, security both emotional and
material, artistic endeavour, talents, careers, contracts and
agreements in business, new opportunity, deep sea travel and
artistic triumphs and expansion. The suit of Deniers or Pentacles refers to financial transactions, material gain, wind-
falls, the inheritance of unearned money, legal matters pertaining to money and all things material but impermanent.

THE SUIT OF CUPS

Pertaining to love, success, happiness, protection, social matters, abundance.

KING. A professional man, in the Church or connected with law, he is warm hearted, sympathetic, sensitive and creative, and a good husband. This man is a man of ideas, skilled in the ways of the world. He always looks after himself first. He can represent a negotiator in favour of the client.

QUEEN. The loved one or mistress, she is a highly artistic woman, romantic, slightly fey and prophetic, very sensitive and a visionary. This card can also mean a good mixer, love and a happy marriage.

KNIGHT. A single young bachelor, he is a refined, artistic, high-principled man and may be a lover, a seducer or a rival in love. He can also denote a pleasant visit or a proposition, a message, advances, an invitation, or the bearer of a message.

KNAVE. News, a message, the birth of a child, new methods in business, a willing and a helpful youth who gives good advice or is of a quiet, artistic and meditative nature are all shown by this card.

ACE. The Ace means passion, inspiration, love, joy, and spiritual nourishment, replenishment. It can mean love, marriage and motherhood. This is the card of feminine gestation

REG.DI COPPE

The Queen of Cups

FAN.DI COPPE

The Knave of Cups

83

The Ace of Cups

The Three of Cups

of the Minor Arcana signifying faith, fruitful abundance, creative talent, enterprise in creation, good news, gay company. When near the love cards this means either true love or great rewards from a loving union.

TWO. The two means partnership, loving union, friendship, the reconciliation of opposites, the resolution of quarrels, the end of rivalry, the signing of a contract or treaty, and wealth, but restriction.

THREE. Emotional growth, liaison, a love affair, happiness and fulfilment in marriage, fruition, maternity, comfort, trust, happy issue, conclusion of a happy matter, a healing of wounds, congratulations and rejoicing are all shown by the Three.

FOUR. The Four reveals outside meddling in matters of the heart, hostile influence, discontent with prevailing circumstances and environment leading to a fresh evaluation of material success and a seeking of new paths. The 'divine discontent' card – when badly aspected this card means boredom, and also timidity in pursuing new paths.

FIVE. Inheritance, gifts, an old life finished, something lost – this card means regret for a wrong choice or past actions, new alternatives to be explored when something is lost or finished, disappointment in marriage, or a love affair gone wrong.

SIX. This is a card of conflict and reconciliation, the results of past action and influences evidencing themselves in the present. Something begins now which has its

84

roots in the past – past efforts bringing present rewards. An old friend or lover appears, or a long-held dream or a love affair with roots in the past is realized. When badly aspected this card means that the client lives too much in the past.

SEVEN. There is an exceptional choice to be made and much care and consideration must be given. Imagination, dreams, and mental activity are shown by this 'Castles in Spain' card, as are creative inspiration, mystical experience, the unexpected, a surprise to do with mental or creative activity. If badly aspected this person has too many interests and should settle to one main activity.

EIGHT. Leaving the past behind, new experiences, new friends, new activities, leaving a place or abandoning a situation, a change of attitude through disillusion or suffering, a person 'refined by the flame to rise like a phoenix': all these may be indicated by the Eight.

NINE. The 'wish card' signifies the total fulfilment of one paramount desire, as well as generosity, kindliness, good health and success, and stability both emotional and material.

TEN. This card, pertaining to property or a residence, also means honour, fame, publicity and prestige, the love of friends, lasting success. It denotes work to do with the public, and also peace of mind and prosperity.

THE SUIT OF STAVES, WANDS OR CLUBS

REG. DI BASTONI

The Queen of Staves

CAV. DI BASTONI

The Knight of Staves

Pertaining to the professions, property, consolidation, the arts, new ventures, stability and success.

KING. A dark man, honest, upright, generous and strong, possibly a family man, he gives good impartial advice and sympathy. He also means successful business dealings and an unexpected heritage.

QUEEN. A woman of medium dark colouring of friendly, generous and tolerant disposition, a home and country lover, she is independent, protective and makes a good friend. She also means a successful business transaction and new enterprises.

KNIGHT. This card means a young man, medium dark, and is also the 'intuition card', as well as the card which can mean emigration. It denotes flight, change of residence, departure, also conflict and rivalry in business if badly aspected, and can sometimes mean good stable sense in money matters.

KNAVE. The Knave can be the bearer of a message from a loved one: a postman, a messenger, or an adaptable bright young person of either sex. He means good news, or stimulating news pertaining to finances. This card can also, when placed next to a male court card, mean honours or good news about a child.

The Ace of Staves

The Five of Staves

ACE. The Ace indicates a new undertaking, also a new foundation for success, artistic inspiration, wisdom, innovation, creation, abundance, a new cycle of creative activity, the founding of a family, or the basis for founding a fortune.

TWO. Intellectual work, courage and initiative overcoming obstacles, high motives, tolerance, justice, wisdom, scientific men in a high place giving help, authority and success through strength and vision – the two of staves can be any of these.

THREE. Partnership brings wealth and fame. The Three can also signify enterprises, a good star, help from a powerful friend, original ideas, powerful convictions, good powers of expression, rewards from work of an inspirational nature, an artist or inventor who turns dreams into reality, a trade partnership, or efforts rewarded.

FOUR. The card of the successful designer or inventor, it shows the professional realm of ideas allied to the beauty of perfected work, and also a pause in activities, a peaceful tranquil period away from the demands of society, romance, the family bond, harmony and the 'Harvest Home'.

FIVE. A struggle in love and in life is indicated: love triumphs over obstacles. Mental ability is needed to avoid defeat. It may mean overcoming obstacles, then a change for the better after the struggle.

SIX. The fulfilment of hopes and wishes in one's career, wonderful news, victory over a situation, diplomacy overcoming opposition, achievement and great satisfaction are shown by the six.

SEVEN. A successful change in profession is assured but strength and determination are needed to achieve success. Opposition is defeated through sustained effort and great courage. The Seven also signifies dissemination of knowledge, writing, lecturing, teaching: it is the 'teacher' card.

EIGHT. The Eight indicates the time to be up and doing something new, the end of a period of calm or the end of a delay, approaching a goal, taking a journey, haste in travel, movement, news coming quickly, overseas travel or overseas connections – and the arrows of love.

NINE. This card is better than the nine of cups, the 'wish card'; it is the strongest in the pack and brings a safe and unassailable position. It brings success particularly in the fields of the arts or the professions. It can denote advice given or taken, expansion, balanced judgement, honesty, integrity, courage in defence, strength in reserve and victory through strength and integrity.

TEN. The card of consolidation, it pertains to big business, new contracts, new ventures or an overseas journey or trip to a strange place. It can also mean a burden soon to be lifted, or a problem about to be solved. If badly aspected, it can mean power used unwisely, force triumphant, narrow-minded fixed ideas.

THE SUIT OF DENIERS OR PENTACLES

Pertaining to all money matters, litigation and material wealth.

KING. He indicates a fair man, possibly inarticulate and uneducated, but intuitive, patient, wise and loyal. He has a mathematical bent. Disinterested, he could be unsympathetic, has a slow, deliberate turn of mind, and is stable and cautious. He would make a good parent but a bad enemy.

QUEEN. A fair-headed woman, possibly of independent means, she is materialistic, practical and loves the good things of life. The card has the connotation of money-making, wealth and responsibility to wealth.

KNIGHT. A young man, he could be a new acquaintance, or could mean an indiscretion with the opposite sex. The young man is materialistic, leans to established forms of authority, is traditional, persevering and has a code of honour. This card can also mean the coming and going of a matter, or laborious work, and much patience needed to see it through.

KNAVE. This card can mean a message containing good news, or a letter with money in it. The knave is a young fair boy or girl, avaricious and materialistic, but diligent. This card also means respect for learning, new opinions, new ideas and scholarship.

ACE. The Ace can show the begin-

RE DI DANARI

The King of Deniers

CAV. DI DANARI

The Knight of Deniers

89

The Ace of Deniers

The Six of Deniers

ning of an enterprise that will bring monetary reward. Gifts, legacies, the appreciation of beauty on a physical plane, materialistic comfort, gold, prosperity, luxury, love of possessions, sensuousness, endurance, stoicism, security based on a firm foundation – the Ace of Pentacles can signify all these.

TWO. The Two means fluctuation in fortune, the need for skilful manipulation to achieve success, imminent change, harmony in the midst of change, new moves, and news pertaining to journeys, communication, success in one direction, the use of one talent to achieve success, or gifts coming.

THREE. The Three can betoken professionalism and craftsmanship, success after training, or hard work and consistent effort. It can also indicate a good time for business expansion, skill in trade, artistry, success, help, co-operation, renown through ability, esteem, honour and glory.

FOUR. Possessions and material acquisitiveness are shown by the Four as are obstacles and problems of financial nature, the establishment of a business or commercial firm, inheritance, a legacy – and miserly tendencies, if badly aspected.

FIVE. 'Needs must when the devil drives'. The head ruled by the heart brings sorrow: the Five can mean love gone astray, enforced restrictions, spiritual loneliness; if badly aspected, homesickness, loss of security or loss of position in life.

SIX. The theatrical or entertainment card of the Minor

90

Arcana, it means help from above, or help from a generous person, just rewards, money affairs put on a stable footing, sympathy, kindness and charity. When unfavourably situated this means a lawsuit over money.

SEVEN. The Seven can signify a gift or sudden gain. 'Procrastination is the thief of time': it is a warning to work consistently, for past efforts will only be successful through consistent effort. It is the card of barter, loan and money, but with a possibility of delay. This card could also mean a potential suitor, or results from the past bearing fruit.

EIGHT. The Eight indicates a change that will bring material benefits. The 'talent card' allied with energy, it may presage turning skills into a profession or money earned through talent or skill, possible employment to come but in a new skilled field, beginning again, or the reward of labour.

NINE. A substantial income earned through effort and thrift and material wealth may be meant by the Nine. The reward for effort and sound administration, the successful completion of something resulting in rewards and comfort, and the solution to a problem are also possible meanings.

TEN. The ten covers everything pertaining to the house and family: a purchase or sale, establishing a family tradition, reverence for history, tradition and a settled way of life, money spent on a house, buying or selling, blood ties and inheritance, property concerns, dowries and legacies.

THE SUIT OF SWORDS

Pertaining to the struggles of the spirit, competition, battle, strife, striving and growing, and loneliness.

KING. Possibly a dark man of authority, or an intellectual with strong moral conviction, he can be a severe critic, and often is a legal man or counsellor. He could be an innovator, but is often found in government, the armed forces or the legal profession.

QUEEN. A woman possibly dark and often in authority, she is self-reliant and strong. This is the widow's card, and it carries with it a sense of sadness and privation. She makes a good friend but a bad enemy. This card also denotes the struggle of spirit over material concerns, or can denote attention to detail.

KNIGHT. A dark impetuous man or a mischief-maker of either sex may enter the client's life for good or ill. It also means a fighter, a person who is at his best in a difficult situation, or skill in defence and courage in struggle and combat. It can mean a struggle yet to come, or if near cards meaning illness can denote the surgeon.

KNAVE. This card can mean inner conflict which is the result of past injustices, possibly during childhood, an unscrupulous rival in business, or a deceitful person who carries tales, or spies; it can also mean scrutiny or a diplomatic messenger who will nego-

RE DI SPADE

The King of Swords

FAN. DI SPADI

The Knave of Swords

tiate business.

The Ace of Swords

ACE. The symbol of strength in adversity and triumph over great odds, it can be the sword of Damocles or the symbol of divine justice. Just rewards are indicated, or a sense of the inevitable, something which is beginning and which cannot be stopped, but will change the entire life. 'The old order changeth'. This is a card of great force for either good or ill, for love or hate. It means victory after conquest.

TWO. The stalemate: this is the card of balanced forces, meaning help and friendship in adversity, good coming out of evil, a sense of equilibrium. If badly aspected this card means impotence and indecision.

THREE. This card can mean a severing of ties, breaking up a partnership or a marriage, a permanent or temporary separation. It always means disruption or upheaval, such as sorrow and tears over a faithless lover, but it always carries the sense of clearing the ground for something new, 'the darkest hour before the dawn'.

The Four of Swords

FOUR. A voluntary period of quiet is possible after a test or battle. It can also mean firm administration pertaining to law, peace and order after struggle and chaos, occultism, mediation, religion, rest. It can mean hospitalization and convalescence, or merely a period of quiet for thinking things through.

FIVE. The client must learn to accept the inevitable, acknowledge defeat and swallow false pride in order to build on more secure foundations, or proceed in a new direction. It can mean a narrow escape from physical danger, or a threat averted, but it usually denotes the acceptance of limitations before moving upwards and onwards.

SIX. This is the card of travel or flight, usually denoting a change to a more pleasing environment, or position. It also means success after worry or anxiety, or the removal of a large obstacle after a period of strain. It could also denote an overseas visitor or the taking of risks which would turn out favourably.

SEVEN. 'Softly softly catchee monkey' . . . this card denotes the necessity for prudence and evasion in order to gain an objective. The use of brain not brawn is indicated, and direct or aggressive tactics would be disastrous. It can denote partial success or uncertain hope, and possibly the danger of injury while travelling or when indulging in sport.

EIGHT. This is the card which means the bonds will soon be broken and the restrictions lifted, but patience and attention to detail will be needed to avoid criticism. Perhaps there is doubt as to which direction to take, but a sign will come to lead the way.

NINE. This card can mean a difficult choice entailing suffering and sacrifice or the death of a loved one, bringing sorrow and desolation, as well as patient suffering borne with fortitude. It can mean a road accident or loss, if badly aspected.

TEN. This card can be taken on two levels, the national and the personal. It can mean the lowest point in a nation's economy, or the lowest ebb of human affairs. It can also denote self-honesty, the beginnings of seeing a dream, infatuation, relationship or illusion for what it's really worth; it can, if badly aspected, mean sudden misfortune, pain and even ruin and if near JUSTICE and THE DEVIL can denote imprisonment. But on a spiritual plane it can mean the end of the darkness and the beginning of light.

SOME DIFFERENT COMBINATIONS OF
THE MINOR ARCANA

FOUR ACES. A favourable chance leads to a new life.

THREE ACES. Artistic success comes with something new.

TWO ACES. If red, marriage; if black, a new project or contracts are to be expected.

FOUR KINGS. This means a great honour, and often public acclaim.

THREE KINGS. They mean important consultations and contracts.

TWO KINGS. Professional advice or specialist medical counsel is indicated.

FOUR QUEENS. Scandal, publicity or a great debate are meant.

THREE QUEENS. They refer to a public gathering or a public discussion.

TWO QUEENS. A sincere friendship is shown.

FOUR KNIGHTS. This means police or law courts.

THREE KNIGHTS. This means the armed forces, workmen around the house, or noisy conviviality.

TWO KNIGHTS. Lawyers or doctors consult.

FOUR KNAVES. Sudden news of the serious illness of a friend comes.

THREE KNAVES. A fight or a quarrel is revealed.

TWO KNAVES. Young people cause worry.

FOUR TENS. Sudden news bringing good fortune.

THREE TENS. Hasty travel or news from overseas is shown.

TWO TENS. This means change of residence.

FOUR NINES. It means a new life or alternatively a good friend gives help.

THREE NINES. Marked success is indicated, particularly if spades are absent.

TWO NINES. They mean a gift.

FOUR EIGHTS. A parting, or a mixed success resulting in a parting, are meant.

THREE EIGHTS. They betoken marriage, or an addition to the family.

TWO EIGHTS. New surroundings, new knowledge, new studies are indicated.

FOUR SEVENS. This means the birth either of a person or of an artistic conception.

THREE SEVENS. News of illness, or illness to the client are revealed.

TWO SEVENS. A sudden surprising gift comes.

AUGUR   A priest in ancient Rome who studied the flight and migratory habits of birds and predicted the course of events from such study.

CADUCEUS   A cosmic magical and astronomical symbol, depending upon its application. The wand of Hermes, or Mercury, it originally featured a triple-headed serpent with the property of inducing sleep, but modern medicine, in adopting it as a symbol, uses only two serpents, one black and one white, to signify disease and cure and has the two wings of Mercury on top.

CHARMS AND TALISMANS   These are magical notes on formulae which can be drawn, written, recited or sung over an object in order to imbue it with certain magical properties and powers, believed to effect a desired result or state of being. These objects could be of any material substance, but the most common were talismans, amulets and lucky stones. The amulets or bracelets were often worn to ward off the Evil Eye or evil spirits and give protection, while the talismans were sometimes worn, either as inscribed parchment or cloth, as a pendant hanging from a chain, to endow the wearer with certain powers, strengths or abilities.

COSMIC   The definition of cosmic in the Rosicrucian manual is 'The Divine Infinite Intelligence or the Supreme Being Permeating Everything, the Creative Forces of God'.

COSMIC CONSCIOUSNESS   That super-awareness, possessed by very few, of the life-pattern of the universe and the ultimate goal of the ever-developing spirit.

COSMIC LEMNISCATE   A figure shaped like an eight lying on its side which the ancient Egyptians believed represented the eternal cosmic forces, for it had neither end nor beginning.

CULT   A series of rituals and practices built into a corporate body of belief which is devoted to the worship of one particular divine concept or divine being.

DEMI-URGE   The force which created all matter, in the Gnostic creed. The inferior, evil, the material element, as opposed to the divine, superior creator of the spirit.

DIANA   The Roman goddess of the moon and the hunt, and the ruler of wild animals. Often equated with the Greek goddess Artemis.

DRUIDS A magical people who practised their rites in a wide domain covering France, England and Ireland, and were very powerful among the Celtic races before the advent of Christianity. They were skilled in all kinds of magic, astrology and alchemy.

EARTH MOTHER Many of the most powerful goddesses in the pantheons of the polytheistic religions were so styled because of their supposed power over the forces of nature.

ESOTERIC Secret traditions: facts usually not accessible to the uninitiated, usually pertaining to secret doctrine, secret rites and secret philosophy. When made public the facts become exoteric.

ENLIGHTENMENT The knowledge of God achieved through spiritual development.

THE THREE FATES Clotho the spinner, Lachesis the disposer and Atropos, the unchangeable, who snips the thread of life.

FEMININE PRINCIPLE The feminine principle, or feminine force, in occult lore represents one part of the cosmic pattern – the passive, negative, receptive and regenerative aspects which are always considered feminine in quality. The female goddesses in the pantheons usually stood for the material and physical forces of nature, nourishment and intuitive wisdom.

GOAT OF MENDES Usually depicted with four horns, this figure derives from an Egyptian deity, a form of Pan. Later it was associated with black magic and as the 'bachelor,' was the goat-like body which the Devil was supposed to assume on the witches' sabbath when he came down to earth and had intercourse with the witches. He was then known as the Sabbatic Goat. Also, this figure became known as a Baphomet, which was the word for an idol of any kind, but which possibly derived from statues fashioned for the cults who worshipped Saturn, Mithras or Dionysus. Most of these portrayed Saturn in many guises, one of which was a horned figure with a beard.

GNOSTICISM Derived from the Greek word for knowledge, it was a creed composed of many elements from the philosophies and beliefs of Babylon, India, Persia and Egypt and embodies as well some of the elements of the Hebrew

Qabbala and the Christian religion. The Gnostic priests practised astrology, numerology and the arts of magic, and some sects appear to have celebrated the Greek mysteries in a slightly debased form. They flourished in the Roman Empire at the time of Christ, their headquarters being Alexandria.

GRIMOIRE A general expression used to cover those books containing information, spells, incantations and alchemical experiments often used in early centuries against the Qabbala and later written to promote Devil worship, and giving instructions for Devil worship.

GYPSIES A contraction of the word Egyptian, but not pertaining to Egypt but rather to Palestine or 'Little Egypt' from where it was believed the wandering tribes of people came. They were gifted with clairvoyance as well as the ability to cast spells, possessed the Evil Eye, and were versed in all kinds of magic.

HECATE Queen of the night, the Dark Moon who brought madness to those who defied her and who guarded the gates of Hades. She commanded all the magical powers of nature, and ruled sorcery and magic.

HERMES TRISMEGISTOS Hermes, messenger of the gods, also identified with the ibis-headed Egyptian god Thoth, inventor of the magical arts and of the art of writing, god of wisdom and patron of the arts. Said to have conceived the *Book of Thoth* or *Book of the Dead*, a collection of magical writings found on papyri, as well as in tombs and on monuments. These were neo-Platonic astrological and alchemical works.

HIEROPHANT A teacher, an adept who has attained the status and experience requisite for the imparting of sacred esoteric knowledge to others.

ISIS Wife of Osiris, she was the greatest of all ancient Egyptian goddesses and had many facets. Some of her titles included 'she who is the beginning', 'she who is without end', 'mistress of magic', 'speaker of the spells', 'the only true bestower of Life'. Her influence was very wide, particularly around the Mediterranean and the Egyptian mysteries commemorating the death and resurrection of Osiris, which still exist in some forms to this day.

JANUS Roman two-headed god of doorways, and later god of beginnings.

JUNO Wife of Jupiter, queen of the Roman gods, ruler of marriage and chastity.

JUPITER King of the Roman gods, identified with the Zeus of the Greeks and with Ammon of Egypt.

KABALA or QABBALA A leading theosophical system of the Hebrews, evolved during the Middle Ages, of mystical spells, rituals and incantations, which was outlawed by the orthodox religion. It was based on an occult interpretation of the Bible and was handed down in an esoteric tradition to students of the occult.

KEY OF SOLOMON A magical *Grimoire* or collection of writings said to have been written by King Solomon, but believed to have been written in either the fourteenth or fifteenth centuries.

KISMET The Arabic word for fate. Moslems believe that a man's life is fated and the course is inevitable.

LAUREL A tree whose leaf has long been considered magical. It symbolized divinity and favour of the gods. Sacred to Venus, it was considered to be a protection against evil spirits. It also denoted royalty, victory and power, and ancient Romans believed that to dream of a laurel wreath presaged national fame and high honours.

LIGHTNING Forked lightning was considered to be a symbol of sacred power.

MALE PRINCIPLE The masculine force: in occult lore, the active, positive aspect of the cosmic law and pattern.

MANDALA A psychic symbol denoting wholeness. Usually of a circular shape, with a symbol of the self in the centre and other symbols at each corner.

MITHRAISM This cult, open only to the masculine sex, was very popular in the Roman Empire, particularly with the army, although it originated in Persia. The god hero Mithras gave up his life on earth to service of mankind and later, upon his ascension to heaven, he continued to exert his influence among his followers in their struggle against evil. The Mithraists practised elaborate initiation ceremonies which were graded in seven stages, corresponding to their seven grades of heaven which culminated in the dwelling of the Ineffable.

THE MUSES The nine daughters of Zeus and Mnemosyne. Each muse ruled over an art or science and they gave divine inspiration to the poet, painter and author.

THE MYSTERIES In these ancient rites, the priests, initiates and neophytes acted in allegorical tableaux that featured the deities, the secret significance of which was explained to the initiates upon their gaining their 'crown', or after passing the Dionysian mystery cult.

THE DIONYSIAN MYSTERY CULT This cult originated in Phrygia and began as an orgiastic celebration, with the sacrifice of animals and the drinking of blood. Later these rites took on a deeper, more spiritual significance, and were called the Orphic mysteries. They incorporated belief in reincarnation.

THE ELEUSIAN MYSTERIES This was the oldest of the mystery cults which originated nine hundred years before Christ in Eleusis. It was centred around the 'earth mother', Demeter and her daughter Persephone, the regenerating principle, and was agrarian in character.

NEOPHYTE A new convert, a novice.

OSIRIS The husband of Isis, the father of Horus, worshipped as the maker of heaven and earth.

PAN The all-encompassing: associated with Priapus and, later, the Maypole, he was a cloven-hoofed, horned and primitive prototype of the 'all father'. Pan was the god of hunting and of forests, and patron of shepherds, who embodied the primitive forces of nature.

PERSEPHONE Daughter of Demeter, the 'earth mother' and wife of Hades, the king of hell, who was returned to her mother for eight months in every year.

PHRYGIAN CAP Sacred to the Rosicrucians, always red in colour, it is said to be phallic in origin, deriving from circumcision. Possibly derives from an ancient representation of Hermes, who was depicted wearing a herdsman's cap of a similar shape. The magician is sometimes shown wearing a cap like this.

ROSE Sacred to Venus and used in love potions this flower has been regarded by many cultures as sacred and a symbol of life, love and beauty. The Greeks regarded it as a sign of silence, and it was used as a decoration in the robes of the initiate in the crowning ceremony in the mysteries.

SHAMAN Shamanism is the primitive belief in discarnate intelligence or in spirits whose priests or medicine men practised rites which they believed gave them the power over or the control of such spirits so that they could exorcise them or command them to appear. It is used now in a general sense to describe any application of methods of magic in order to communicate with or control unseen forces considered to be supernatural or superhuman.

SISTRUM The sacred rattle of Isis, always denoting joy and merriment.

TITANS In Greek mythology, a race of giants who attacked and fought the gods for supremacy.

UNICORN The beautiful mythical creature famed for its magical ability, associated with the moon and the female element. It was small and white, looked rather like a beautiful horse and had one curled horn in the middle of its forehead. It could only be lured and captured by a virgin, who would sit in a wood where it would trustfully approach her and put its head in her lap.

Bibliography

Aupelius, Lucius, *The Golden Ass* (Trans. Robert Graves), Penguin, 1950.

Bennett, Sidney, *Tarot for the Millions*, Sherborne Press, California, 1970.

Brown, Wenzell, *How to Tell Fortunes with Cards*, Oak Tree Press, 1963.

Douglas, Alfred, *The Tarot*, Gollancz, 1972.

Gardner, Richard, *The Tarot Speaks*, Rigel Press, London, 1971.

Huson, Paul, *The Devil's Picture Book*, Abacus Books, 1972.

Marple, Eric, *The Dark World of Witches*, Robert Hale, 1962.

Ouspensky, P. D., *A New Model of the Universe*, Routledge and Kegan Paul, 1949.

Pushong, Carlyle A., *The Tarot of the Magi*, Regency Press, 1967.

Rakoczi, Basil Ivan, *The Painted Caravan*, Boucher, The Hague, 1954.

Shah, Idries, *The Secret Lore of Magic*, Abacus Books, 1957.

Tindall, Gillian, *A Handbook of Witches*, Arthur Baker, 1965.

Waite, A. E., *A Pictorial Key to the Tarot*, Rider, 1971.

Yates, Francis A., *The Art of Memory*, Routledge and Kegan Paul, 1966.

Fontana Books

Fontana is best known as one of the leading paperback publishers of popular fiction and non-fiction. It also includes an outstanding, and expanding, section of books on history, natural history, religion and social sciences.

Most of the fiction authors need no introduction. They include Agatha Christie, Hammond Innes, Alistair MacLean, Catherine Gaskin, Victoria Holt and Lucy Walker. Desmond Bagley and Maureen Peters are among the relative newcomers.

The non-fiction list features a superb collection of animal books by such favourites as Gerald Durrell and Joy Adamson.

All Fontana books are available at your bookshop or newsagent; or can be ordered direct. Just fill in the form below and list the titles you want.
